Further Praise for *Kitchen Yarns*

"In this cozy read, Hood shares recipes that shaped her . . . and the poignant life lessons about loss, love, and friendship she learned in the kitchen." —Nora Horvath, *Real Simple*

"A must-give book for any cooks in your life. . . . A charming and heartfelt collection of personal essays, all centered on the thread of food." —Lauren Daley, *South Coast Today*

"[Hood] never pulls back from writing with searing honesty— even about painful topics."
—Laurie Higgins, *Cape Cod Times*

"At the end of *Kitchen Yarns*, you may empathize with Hood's sadness, but you will not be disheartened. You will just want to rinse out the pan and start over."
—Betty J. Cotter, *Providence Journal*

"Moving. . . . Hood's sharp essays emphasize food as emotional nourishment, bringing family and friends together— both to celebrate the joys and heal the wounds of life."
—*Publishers Weekly*

"From the first page to the last, readers know they are in the hands of a master storyteller. . . . Full of humor and love, overflowing with heart and life, *Kitchen Yarns* is a beautiful read."
—*Book Reporter*

"A full plate of heart and hearty eats."   *—Kirkus Reviews*

"This warm, humorous, touching, and wonderfully readable book will appeal to food lovers and fans of culinary biographies."
                                        —Library Journal, starred review

"Eminently readable, *Kitchen Yarns*, Ann Hood's tender, witty, and funny voyage through a life of food, reminds us that the visceral taste memories of our past are essential benchmarks of our life, and that the stories of a family are always best felt and expressed through those dishes."
          —Jacques Pépin, world-renowned chef and author of
                                    Heart & Soul in the Kitchen

Kitchen
Yarns

ALSO BY ANN HOOD

Morningstar: Growing Up with Books

The Book That Matters Most

An Italian Wife

The Obituary Writer

The Red Thread

Comfort: A Journey Through Grief

The Knitting Circle

An Ornithologist's Guide to Life

Somewhere Off the Coast of Maine

EDITED BY ANN HOOD

Knitting Pearls

Knitting Yarns

Kitchen Yarns

Notes on Life,
Love, and
Food

ANN HOOD

W. W. NORTON & COMPANY
Independent Publishers Since 1923

Pages 114–15: *Christopher Kimball's Milk Street* Guacamole recipe courtesy Christopher Kimball.

Page 126: Li-Young Lee, excerpt from "From Blossoms" from *Rose*. Copyright © 1986 by Li-Young Lee. Reprinted with permission of The Permissions Company, Inc., on behalf of BOA Editions, Ltd., www.boaeditions.org.

Printed in the United States of America
First published as a Norton paperback 2019

For information about permission to reproduce selections from this book, write to Permissions, W. W. Norton & Company, Inc., 500 Fifth Avenue, New York, NY 10110

For information about special discounts for bulk purchases, please contact W. W. Norton Special Sales at specialsales@wwnorton.com or 800-233-4830

Manufacturing by Sheridan Books, Inc.
Book design by Chris Welch
Production manager: Lauren Abbate

Library of Congress Cataloging-in-Publication Data

Names: Hood, Ann, 1956–
Title: Kitchen yarns : notes on life, love, and food / Ann Hood.
Description: First edition. | New York : W. W. Norton & Company, independent publishers since 1923, [2018]
Identifiers: LCCN 2018027425 | ISBN 9780393249507 (hardcover)
Subjects: LCSH: Cooking. | Hood, Ann, 1956– | Novelists, American—20th century—Biography. | LCGFT: Cookbooks.
Classification: LCC TX714 .H6573 2018 | DDC 641.5—dc23
LC record available at https://lccn.loc.gov/2018027425

ISBN 978-0-393-35753-0 pbk.

W. W. Norton & Company, Inc., 500 Fifth Avenue, New York, N.Y. 10110
www.wwnorton.com

W. W. Norton & Company Ltd., 15 Carlisle Street, London W1D 3BS

1 2 3 4 5 6 7 8 9 0

For Michael

and

in memory of Gogo

September 5, 1931–February 24, 2018

Contents

Introduction

I grew up eating. A lot. As the great food writer M. F. K. Fisher said, "First we eat, then we do everything else." That describes my childhood home. In my mind, my Italian grandmother, Mama Rose, was always cooking. We lived with her in the house she moved to with her parents when they came from Conca Della Compania, a small, mountainous town an hour and a world away from Naples, Italy, to West Warwick, Rhode Island. When I was young, Mama Rose and her mother, Nonna, kept an enormous garden in the backyard, and they would sit on summer afternoons and snap the ends off string beans (served cold with garlic and mint), press tomatoes into sauce, pickle red and green peppers for the Christmas antipasto. We had fruit trees—Seckel pear, cherry, apple, fig—and blueberry and raspberry bushes. They raised rabbits and chickens, too. More than once a beloved white bunny—Snowball, Snowflake, Snowy—disappeared from its cage only for us to have funny-tasting "chicken" that night at dinner.

My mother baked pies—lemon meringue and chocolate cream—and a fancy Friday night dinner of creamed tuna on toast, but otherwise she left the cooking to Mama Rose, who pretty much banned us kids from her kitchen, which was the smallest room in a house of small rooms. So small that the refrigerator didn't fit in it and stood instead right by the dining room table. How she fed so many people—as many as thirty on Sundays and holidays—in a kitchen with no countertops and just a four-burner electric stove, I don't know. But she did, turning out homemade gnocchi, polenta with kale or red sauce and sausage, gallons of spaghetti sauce, and hundreds of meatballs. For reasons I never knew, we called that little kitchen "the pantry," and the room others might call a dining room "the kitchen." We kids would sit in the kitchen at the green-and-brown enamel-topped table, with its pattern of sheaves of wheat, to mix the ground beef, egg, parsley, garlic, and bread crumbs for the meatballs. That was the closest we came to getting any cooking lessons. Mostly, we were told to get out of Mama Rose's way so that she could cook.

My father manned the grill, as most fathers did in the 1960s. He turned out thick T-bone steaks, hamburgers and hot dogs, Italian sausages, and his two specialties: Chicken Bountiful, which was half a chicken topped with potatoes and green beans and cream of celery soup and wrapped in tinfoil, and shish kebabs, which were chunks of steak marinated in his secret sauce. We weren't allowed to help at the grill, either, and really, who wanted to? Grilling happened on summer weekends, and we wanted nothing more than to run through the sprinkler in our bathing suits, drink cold soda, or sit in front of the fan watching television.

All of this is to say that even though I lived in a house filled with good food, no one ever taught me to cook. In 1979, I was working as a TWA flight attendant, based in Boston, and I lived in a tall apartment building that overlooked the bay. I was usually away on trips, flying to San Francisco or Las Vegas. When I was home, I mostly ate out with some combination of my five roommates—at Regina Pizzeria in the North End, TGI Fridays on Exeter Street, Durgin-Park or Cricket's at Faneuil Hall. One day I found myself alone in the apartment, a rare experience with so many roommates. I remember enjoying the pleasure of drinking coffee in my little twin bed and not having to talk to anyone, give love advice, or hear complaints about passengers. By noon, I was hungry. If my mother didn't send me home after a visit to Rhode Island with a lasagna or a bag of meatballs, I had nothing to eat. So I dressed and went to Faneuil Hall, where I ordered a ham and cheese sandwich from one of the shops there.

"Eleven dollars," the woman said as she handed me a white bag with my sandwich and a pickle inside.

"Eleven dollars!" I shrieked. Or maybe I didn't say it out loud. All I know is that I made a vow to never again pay that much for something I could surely make myself.

A friend had given me *Betty Crocker's Cookbook* for my college graduation the year before, and I methodically worked my way through those recipes, ruining more dinners than I can count. Soon I was clipping recipes from the newspaper and buying other cookbooks—*Moosewood, Laurel's Kitchen, The New York Times 60-Minute Gourmet.* Over the next few years, I taught myself to cook. Sometimes I reached too far—stuffed pork chops with apple compote, whole wheat pizza that I could have used for a doorstop. But slowly I learned how to make an omelet and scramble eggs, use leftover chicken for curried chicken salad, make a stock from the chicken bones.

By the time I was married and raising a family, I was a good home cook. As in the household in which I grew up, life at my house revolved around the kitchen. Something was always simmering or roasting or marinating. But unlike in my childhood home, my kids stood on stools right beside me, sprinkling shredded Gruyère on potatoes for an au gratin, layering slices of apples for a crisp, whipping cream, or chopping vegetables. One of those kids, my son, Sam, grew up and moved to Brooklyn, where he makes dinners for his friends—Spaghetti Amatriciana or risotto or Chicken Chili. One of those kids, my daughter Grace, died when she was only five, already the expert Apple Crisp maker in our family. One of those kids, my fourteen-year-old daughter, Annabelle, lives with me across town from her father in a loft in a converted factory, where every night I cook her favorite food—roast chicken, rice and peas, homemade macaroni and cheese—and we sit together at our table that my friend Steve made for me and we eat together. "It seems to me," M. F. K.

Fisher wrote, "that our three basic needs, for food and security and love, are so mixed and mingled and entwined that we cannot straightly think of one without the others. So it happens that when I write about hunger, I am really writing about love and the hunger for it."

This is how my culinary life began—in a big, noisy family, in rooms overflowing with people and food, with the rustic peasant food of our village. But even in the midst of this, no one ever taught me how to cook. *Kitchen Yarns* is my journey from that family and that childhood through my early efforts at cooking—flank steak marinated in Good Seasons salad dressing to impress a boy I liked in college; pesto made with two cups of *dried* basil—to diligently copying recipes from *The Silver Palate Cookbook* as a young single woman living in New York City to trying to make the perfect spaghetti carbonara, like the one I ate in Rome on a layover as a TWA flight attendant. Eventually, I became a very good home cook, throwing elaborate dinner parties and cooking in the kitchen with my own children. Today, I'm married to the food writer Michael Ruhlman, who has taught me how to properly dice an onion and make chicken stock in the oven while I sleep, and who mixes me his recipe for whiskey sours at the end of a long day.

I realized as, over the years, I wrote essays about food— Laurie Colwin's Tomato Pie, my father's mac and cheese— that as M. F. K. Fisher said, writing about food is really writing about love. When I write an essay about food, I am really uncovering something deeper in my life—loss, family, confusion, growing up, growing away from what I knew, returning, grief, joy, and, yes, love.

It was impossible to put these essays in chronological order. Like so many things about complicated issues, the themes and settings and time frames overlap, recede, jump forward. I tried to put them in *loose* chronological order, but my adult self and my present self keep having new realizations about my younger self, and so that intrudes on those earlier recollections and stories I tell. They move crookedly from my earliest memories of fried chicken, to the food my mother made when I was a child, to that Spaghetti Carbonara and Silver Palate Chicken Marbella, to my young children, my divorce, my new happy marriage. To me, there is a shape that is not unlike a recipe: it starts at the beginning, but as ingredients are added, it becomes something different. Each essay stands alone, but taken as a whole, they make a life—mine.

Kitchen
Yarns

The Golden Silver Palate

The first time I made pesto sauce, I used dried basil. Lots of it. Two entire containers of McCormick's dried basil, to be exact. This was 1982, and I wanted to impress my new boyfriend. Josh had just relocated to New York City from San Francisco. He made a mean cup of coffee by pressing the grounds through what looked like a sock. He put apples in coleslaw. He bought live soft-shell crabs in Chinatown, fried them in butter, and put them in a sandwich smeared with homemade mayonnaise.

Until I fell in love with Josh, my idea of a fancy dinner came straight out of that orange Betty Crocker cookbook I got as a college graduation present: Chicken Kiev (filled with dried parsley, dried rosemary, dried thyme, and lots of butter), Chicken Rice-A-Roni, and a salad with a sugary dressing poured over lettuce, slivered almonds, and mandarin oranges straight from the can. Back in college, my sorority sisters and I used to marinate flank steak in Good Seasons Italian dressing to woo boys we had crushes on. For dessert, Kathy, the sophisticated one, dumped a can of cherries into a pan, poured brandy on it, and lit the whole thing on fire. This was Cherries Jubilee. I also had a recipe for curried chicken salad that I'd torn from a *Glamour* magazine. I made that when my girlfriends came over for lunch.

Luckily, our little apartment on Avenue C made it impossible to put together any of these dishes. I needed a one-pot meal that required no fancy appliances. So I stirred all of that basil into a bowl of olive oil and crushed garlic, added some Parmigiano-Reggiano, and tossed it with spaghetti, cooked al dente. It is surely a sign of how much Josh loved me that he ate my pesto sauce at all, even as I spit it out, mumbling that it was, well, a little dry. Afterward, as he did the dishes, Josh said, "I wonder if next time you might use fresh basil. That might work better."

Fresh basil? I tried to imagine what that might even look like. I knew my fresh parsley, the curly and the flat. I even knew that the flat was better, the only kind my Italian grandmother ever used. But *fresh basil?*

"Good idea," I said, certain there would be no next time.

FOR ME, JULIA CHILD did not become the kitchen goddess she was to so many Americans until much later in my life, when I already knew how to cook and had grown to love good food. When I was a teenager, Julia Child was a black-

and-white image on public television, cooking up food too fancy for my tastes. By the time I was in my twenties and living in New York City, she had morphed into a Dan Aykroyd skit on *Saturday Night Live*. During a brief misguided vegetarian phase, I made a whole wheat pizza from the 1976 paean to vegetarian cooking *Laurel's Kitchen*, and gazpacho and tabbouleh salad from Mollie Katzen's seminal *Moosewood Cookbook*. When I latched onto the big Cajun food craze, I almost asphyxiated a small group of friends by trying to make blackened something in my studio apartment. It filled with smoke so spicy that even my cats were gasping for air. Other than my beloved Betty Crocker, I had no cooking gurus.

Until the weekend I visited my friend Gilda Povolo in Ann Arbor, Michigan, and she served me grapes rolled in Roquefort cheese, prosciutto-filled pinwheels, and a chicken dinner topped with prunes and olives, followed by bread pudding, all of it so delicious I had seconds and then thirds. Groaning, I asked her where she'd learned to cook like that. Gilda tossed a red-and-white book onto my lap and said, "It's all in here." The book was *The Silver Palate*. And it changed my life.

That chicken, of course, was Chicken Marbella, the dinnerparty staple for every woman who, like me, had never known that herbs came fresh and green, who was just starting to give grown-up dinner parties, who saw herself as urban and sophisticated but needed—was desperate for—a guidebook.

When my Advanced Fiction Writing class came over for an end-of-semester dinner, I made Chili for a Crowd. When Josh and I took a picnic to Central Park on a summer night, before seeing a play, I made Lemon Chicken or Cold Sesame Noodles. When my parents visited, I made phyllo triangles stuffed with spinach and feta by following the simple drawings in the cookbook, rolling and tucking as if my little package were an American flag.

Once I opened those pages, my world expanded. *The Silver Palate*'s recipe for pesto became routine. Fresh basil? Easy. Now I was buying herbs I'd never even heard of before. Fresh tarragon sat in a glass of water by my sink so that I could easily pluck it. In my fridge I always had a big jar of the Silver Palate's vinaigrette to add to my salads. Suddenly, I was a cook. A good cook. Within a few short years, the food-stained pages fell apart, the binding cracked and crumbled. When I replaced that volume, I bought *The Silver Palate Good Times Cookbook*, too, and soon my repertoire expanded even more. Apple Crisp, Stuffed Pork Loin, Pasta with Sausage and Peppers.

One of the most important things *The Silver Palate* did for me was to open me up to all kinds of foods. I began to cook everything. Instead of relying on that red-and-white book, I cooked from recipes torn from newspapers and food magazines; I had recipes scribbled on napkins and scraps of paper; my bookshelves dipped from the weight of cookbooks. As time passed, I used *The Silver Palate* less and other recipes more. Some things, like that Apple Crisp, I had made so often that I no longer even needed to open the book. I knew it by heart.

One day, I sat at my kitchen table in Providence, Rhode

Island, a pad and pen in front of me, trying to decide what to make for an upcoming dinner party. More than a decade had passed since I was that long-haired girl, crazy in love with a boy from San Francisco, living in a tiny walk-up apartment with a bathtub in the kitchen. Now I was married to a businessman, living in a big Victorian house, with a baby crawling at my feet. The dinner party was for three couples I hardly knew. The men had all worked together at summer camp, friends since they were adolescents. Unlike these long-married couples, I was an interloper, a second wife, a writer from New York City. The dinner loomed ominously.

Then it came to me. The dinner-party meal that never failed. The one Gilda Povolo had served to me so long ago, the one I'd re-created dozens of times for so many boyfriends and their families and our friends. I pulled *The Silver Palate* from my bookshelf and found the well-worn recipes easily, those pages so used that the book fell almost magically open to them.

On my pad, I wrote the ingredients I would need: grapes, Roquefort cheese, heavy cream; phyllo dough, spinach, feta; chicken breasts, prunes, green olives; day-old bread, raisins, eggs. That afternoon, I began to cook, barely needing to glance at the recipes as I moved through my oversized kitchen.

The couples arrived. I nervously poured wine, smiled too much, dashed in and out of the kitchen. On one of those furtive trips, I saw a full measuring cup sitting by the stove. I paused. My chicken was happily baking away, the bread pudding beside it. What was in that measuring cup? I lifted it to

my nose and sniffed. The white wine for the Chicken Marbella. I had ruined the dinner. *The Silver Palate* couldn't save
it, or me, now. I opened the oven. The chicken was finished.
The skin nicely browned, the prunes plump, the green olives
juicy. I set it on the counter, wondering if I should add the
wine now. But that would taste too winey. Disappointed, I
placed it on the platter I'd bought in Italy, added the chopped
fresh parsley, and brought it to the table.

I watched everyone as they cut their chicken and brought
it to their lips.

"What is this?" one of the guys asked, surprised.

"Chicken Marbella," I managed to say.

"This is amazing," he said, shoving more into his mouth.

The women were nodding in agreement. People were taking seconds. And thirds. Even without the wine, the Chicken
Marbella was a success. I couldn't ruin it.

Over the next fifteen years, these same couples came to my
house again and again. I have served them spaghetti carbonara from my own recipe. Steak with chimichurri sauce. Beef
tenderloin with blue cheese. I have served my family these
things too, and so much more. Homemade gnocchi. Beef faji-
tas and thick lentil soup and brined pork chops.

But still, there are days when perhaps I feel nostalgic for a
time that was simpler and cooking seemed like a wild adven-
ture. Days when I feel overwhelmed by responsibility and
burden, by the complications of middle age. Days when I
take my third copy of *The Silver Palate* from the shelf and
find the page with Lemon Chicken, or Black Bean Soup, or,

yes, Chicken Marbella. I run my hand over the sticky cookbook. I read the familiar words. I cook.

CHICKEN MARBELLA

Adapted from *The Silver Palate Cookbook*,
by Julee Rosso and Sheila Lukins

One of the best things about this recipe is that you set everything up the night before you want to serve it, which not only keeps you out of the kitchen and sipping cocktails with everyone else but also allows the chicken to soak up all the yummy marinade. Also, you can serve it at room temperature. That means you can bake it before your guests arrive— I always think of it as a perfect dish for a dinner party, though of course it's a lovely meal anytime—and have it all ready, waiting on a pretty platter.

A word of warning: although, as I've just recounted, I have always thought of Chicken Marbella as a no-fail dish, I actually messed it up recently. Once in over thirty years is a pretty good record, but still when it came out less than wonderful, I was shocked. Here's what happened. I fell madly in love with a guy who also happens to be a cook trained by the CIA—not the Central Intelligence Agency but the Culinary Institute of America—and the author of more than twenty cookbooks and books about chefs and the art of cooking. In other words, I was terrified of cooking for him. One night I made him a pretty mediocre *cacio e pepe*, one of the most basic pasta preparations—just cheese and black pepper—which is very hard to make well. You will note that there is no recipe for *cacio e pepe* in this book. The next time I had the misfortune to make him dinner, I decided to forgo something hard and go for easy but dazzling—in other words, Chicken Marbella. I prepped it the night before he arrived and had at the ready the finishing touch of chopped parsley to sprinkle on top. After cocktails and cheese and crackers on the roof, we came back inside for dinner. But my perfect, no-fail Chicken Marbella failed. The chicken wasn't crisp; the sauce was too sweet. In the middle of the night I woke up remembering I'd forgotten to add the olives, which still sat on the kitchen counter, next to the ramekin of chopped parsley.

So do not attempt this recipe if you are madly in love.

Otherwise, it will never fail you.

Serves 10

INGREDIENTS

> *2 to 3 pounds chicken (I like breasts, but mixed parts are*
> *better for dinner parties)*
> *½ cup olive oil*
> *½ cup red wine vinegar*
> *½ cup pitted prunes*
> *½ cup pitted apricots*
> *½ cup capers*
> *½ cup green olives (even the jarred ones with pimientos work*
> *nicely)*

Cloves from one head of garlic, peeled and crushed lightly
with the back of a knife
A scant ¼ cup dried oregano
Salt and pepper to taste
½ cup brown sugar
½ to ⅓ cup white wine
¼ cup chopped flat-leaf parsley

1. The night before serving this dish, put the chicken in the roasting pan you will cook it in and add the olive oil, red wine vinegar, prunes, apricots, capers, olives, garlic, oregano, salt, and pepper. Mix it all up so the chicken is well coated. Using your hands is acceptable, even preferred. Make sure you don't try to cut corners and skip the marinating step. Rosso and Lukins tell us that it is essential to the moistness of the chicken, and I believe them. So should you.

2. The chicken will take about an hour to cook. If you are going to serve it at room temperature (my favorite way), preheat the oven to 350 degrees F around four o'clock the next afternoon. If you want to serve it hot, start the preheating an hour or so before dinner.

3. Mix up the chicken and marinade again, then sprinkle the chicken with the brown sugar and pour the wine around, not over, the chicken.

4. The chicken is done when its juices run clear, in about an hour.

5. Put the chicken with the prunes, apricots, and olives on your prettiest platter. Spoon some of the pan juices on it

and sprinkle with parsley. The rest of the juices can be served separately in your gravy boat.

I like to serve Chicken Marbella with couscous—it soaks up all those juices.

The Best Fried Chicken

I have massaged it with herbs. Bathed it in buttermilk. Immersed it in water, sugar, and salt. Rolled it in corn flakes, panko, seasoned crumbs. I have spent three days tending to it, double-dipping and double-dredging and double-bathing. Ham has been involved. Also, hot pepper flakes. But now I know that the finest way to make fried chicken is to dust it with heavily salted and peppered flour and fry it in lard until crisp. That's the way my father did it, and his mother before him. That's the way they still do it in his part of Indiana, which is to say the southeast corner, whose Hoosiers are more Kentucky than Midwest. But like all children when they grow up, I doubted and questioned him and his chicken. I grew too sophisticated, and turned away from everything I'd once believed to be true. I tasted too many others that had been fried by the likes of Edna Lewis and Sean Brock. I forgot the crunch of that Indiana chicken, its moistness and peppery

kick. I forgot until a yearning for people and things I no longer knew forced me backward, and brought me home.

I have read that Virginia Woolf's earliest memory is of
a close-up view of the pattern of flowers on her mother's
dress on a train trip to St. Ives. The Scottish poet Edwin
Muir's first memory was of his gold-and-scarlet baptism suit.
American historian Henry Adams remembered the yellow
of a kitchen bathed in sunlight. Tolstoy's first memory is of
being swaddled and crying out for freedom. Me, I remember
fried chicken.

I was three, or maybe four, lying on my back in what
we called the *way back* of our green Chevy station wagon,
watching the trees that lined the Blue Ridge Parkway in Virginia speed past. Every weekend we would get in that station
wagon and take a long drive. To the Luray Caverns or Mon-
ticello or a glass factory outlet somewhere in West Virginia.
And always on these day trips there was a picnic, eaten at
a picnic table beneath mountain pines. Always potato salad,
bread and butter, plums and peaches. Always fried chicken.
My brother, Skip, older by five years, tall and solid (our
mother bought his clothes in the husky section at Heck's
department store), wore his hair in a summer buzz cut and
a striped shirt. A Four Seasons song played on the radio—
"Rag Doll" or "Big Girls Don't Cry"—and my mother sang
along softly and off-key from the front seat. My father drove.
His left arm, the one with the tattoo of an eagle in front of a
blazing-red setting sun, rested on the sill of the open window,
and his fine blond hair fluttered in the hot breeze.

We four were displaced. I didn't know it then, but ever since they'd married, a decade earlier, my parents had been moving at the whim of the U.S. Navy, for whom my father was a proud Seabee. They'd lived in Naples, Italy, and Annapolis, Maryland, with long stretches in between when my father was at sea. My mother was homesick for her small hometown in Rhode Island, for the house where her mother still lived, for the nearness of her sisters and brothers, most of them within walking distance of that house on Fiume Street where they'd all been born. I didn't know that she was still grieving the sudden loss of her favorite sister, Ann-Marie, who had died six years earlier during a routine wisdom tooth extraction. I only knew that my mother had those sad brown eyes, and that it wasn't uncommon for me to walk down the long hall of our apartment and find her staring out the window and crying. To me, my world was that apartment in Arlington, Virginia, and my family was the four of us— Mom, Dad, Skip, and me.

So I am on my back in the *way back* of our green Chevy station wagon, and my brother with his buzz cut and striped shirt is beside me, both of our heads on the pillows taken from our beds, and we are staring out at the trees rushing past us. Then the car slows and everything out the window is brilliant blue and green. My father parks and takes a red cooler with a white lid from the back seat. He opens the wide door of the *way back* and we crawl out. My mother, in a pretty red dress, has already hurried to the wooden picnic table, which is painted green. When she sees us spill out of the car, she smiles, and opens the white lid of the cooler, and pulls from it a large yellow bowl.

"Fried chicken," she says.

It is fried chicken made from my father's recipe, which is to say Indiana Fried Chicken. No buttermilk. No spices. No brining. The chicken is simply dusted with heavily salted and peppered flour, then fried in lard. It is crispy and moist and the best fried chicken in the world. I am three years old, wearing a dress covered in a pattern of yellow flowers, running toward my mother. And the world is perfect.

IN HER ESSAY "A Sketch of the Past," Virginia Woolf links the memory of her mother's flowered dress to a memory of lying in bed in the nursery in St. Ives and listening to the sound of the ocean, on that same trip to St. Ives from London. But Woolf admits that the light in the train of this memory is such that the journey was an evening one, which means that it was not on the way *to* St. Ives but rather *from* St. Ives on their return to London. Therefore the memory of lying in bed and listening to the sea can't be right, an inconvenient fact that questions the veracity of her early memories, and their connection to each other. But Woolf wrote, "If life has a base that it stands upon, if it is a bowl that one fills and fills and fills— then my bowl without a doubt stands upon this memory."

What, then, of my own earliest memory, the one on which my own bowl stands? Although this particular picnic on this particular day is not part of my family's lore, what I remember happening later is this: It's dark, and we are heading home to Virginia from wherever we spent the day, still full of fried chicken. The car smells of the lemony moist towelettes my mother carries in her purse for us to wipe our hands with after eating. My brother has fallen asleep beside me, and I am now watching the pattern the streetlights make as we drive past them. The radio is on, and there is a news bulletin: Marilyn Monroe has been found dead by her housekeeper in the bedroom of her Brentwood home. I remember those words. Marilyn Monroe. Dead. Housekeeper. Brentwood home. My mother starts to cry. Skip sits up and asks what happened.

Then there are bright lights, what I now know were the high beams of another car, and they are moving toward us fast, in our lane, hurtling head-on toward us. There is the sound of metal upon metal, of glass breaking, of someone screaming. For an instant, I am airborne, flying above the *way back,* over the back seat, over the front seat, hurtling toward the night. Until my mother catches me like a football someone has tossed her way. My brother, older, heavier, has not been lifted into the air by the collision but, rather, has been thrown hard against the wall of the back seat, breaking several ribs and suffering a concussion. Surely an ambulance arrived and took Skip to the hospital after the car accident. My father probably went with him; my father was the one who swabbed our scrapes with Mercurochrome and put on our Band-Aids and brought us to the ER for stitches and casts. Yet I have no recollection of sirens or ambulances, of waiting—where? by the side of that dark road?—with my mother. All I remember is what came later, back at home: the long stretch of white bandages on Skip's ribs, my mother's terrified expression, my father lifting a glass of Jack Daniel's in his shaking hands.

We were instructed to keep my brother awake all night and check the size of his pupils every hour. Skip grew up without any lingering effects of his injuries. He became a chemical engineer, figuring out how to clean up toxic waste in places like Niagara Falls' Love Canal. But years later, when my brother was thirty and drowned in the bathtub of his Pittsburgh home, my mother would recall that long-ago accident and wonder if it had something to do with whatever mysterious event led to his death. We spend so much of our grief looking for answers to explain what cannot be explained.

MARILYN MONROE DIED on August 5, 1962. I wasn't three; I was five. A five-year-old who could read. In Virginia at that time, a child had to turn six by September 1 in order to enter first grade. My birthday isn't until December, so it was decided that I should go and live with my grandmother in Rhode Island, where a child could start first grade as long as she turned six by December 31. So was I even in the car in Virginia the night Marilyn Monroe died? Or was I in Rhode Island awaiting the first day of school? "Big Girls Don't Cry" didn't come out until November of that year, and "Rag Doll" came out in 1964. Whatever my mother was humming, it couldn't have been either of those songs.

But I want to keep my bowl full of these images, these soft, lovely memories. I want to keep the taste of that fried chicken on my tongue. Not just the fried chicken at that roadside picnic in the Blue Ridge Mountains but years of it: hot from the silver fryolator in a bright yellow bowl, cold in the backyard on a summer day, all you can eat at a chicken place in Indiana with all of my Indiana cousins and aunts and uncles. In my college years, when my friends and I drove to Florida every spring break, my mother fried up chicken for us to snack on during the long drive.

But somehow years passed. All that other fancier, more complicated fried chicken came my way. Then last summer I found myself craving the simple fried chicken of my childhood. No. I found myself craving my father's throaty laugh, the way he said *roof* like it rhymed with *hoof,* how being wrapped in his arms made everything okay. But he was gone almost twenty years, although the particular blue of his eyes had not faded for me. And my brother, dead at thirty, the science geek who had the first Betamax and CD player; what would he think of iPhones and Netflix and everything the world has invented without him? How I wanted to have a beer with both of them, ask their advice on the big life decisions I was facing. And then I craved that fried chicken.

I was heading to a wedding in Michigan that August, and although it was not exactly on my route, I needed to detour to Greensburg, Indiana. I sent out a message to my Hood cousins: *Coming through Greensburg. Want fried chicken.* A flurry of possibilities dropped into my in-box, and finally they settled on the Brau House in Oldenburg. We filled a room there, and in no time platters of all-you-can-eat fried chicken covered the tables. My cousin Keith Hood took me back into the kitchen, where the owner told me how she made that perfect chicken: lots of salt, lots of pepper—more of both than you think you need—in flour. Fry until crispy. So simple, this recipe. There were mashed potatoes and corn too, but it was the fried chicken I'd come for and it was the fried chicken I ate, breast after crispy breast.

Every bite brought me back in time to that rest stop somewhere in Virginia, at a wooden picnic table eating fried chicken made by my mother, with my older brother beside me and my father so young his tattoo is still vivid reds and blues. All of us so young, and happy, and full.

INDIANA FRIED CHICKEN

No offense to Bobby Flay, but he has a recipe for Hoosier fried chicken that is way too fancy and cluttered with buttermilk and eggs and garlic powder. Real Indiana fried chicken has exactly four ingredients: chicken, flour, salt, and pepper. There is no thyme or lemon or anything like that. I am delighted to learn that there is now actually a southeastern Indiana fried chicken tour, and if you happen to be in southeastern Indiana, I highly recommend it. Please stop by Greensburg, the Hood hometown, and take a picture standing in front of the courthouse, where a tree grows out of the roof. You can buy a postcard of it too, and send it to me.

INGREDIENTS

As much chicken as you want
Enough flour to coat all that chicken
Lots of salt
Lots of pepper
Oil to fry the chicken in—enough to cover it

A NOTE ON THE OIL: My father used only lard to fry his chicken, and I suggest you do the same. However, the fine people at the Brau House in Oldenburg, Indiana, told me they use canola oil, and their chicken was among the best I've ever had.

1. Put all that flour in a bowl and mix in more salt and pepper than you think is prudent, then throw it all into a big zip-top bag.
2. Get your oil hot enough for frying, about 350 degrees F.
3. Add the chicken, piece by piece, into the flour, salt, and pepper in the zip-top bag and kind of shake it around. Remove each piece, shaking off the excess, and place on a plate until you've coated enough pieces to fit in the fryer without crowding it, which will lower the temperature.
4. Put the chicken in the hot oil in batches, making sure the pieces don't touch each other, and fry until golden brown, flipping each piece once the bottom looks crunchy. It

should take about 10 minutes for good-sized chicken parts, 8 for smaller ones. If you're a thermometer kind of cook, it should read about 160 degrees F when you insert it into the thickest part of the chicken.

5. Serve warm or at room temperature in a big yellow bowl, if you have one.

Pie Lady

Instead of a diamond engagement ring, my father presented my mother with a sturdy piece of off-white American Tourister luggage. He was in the navy, a Seabee, an Indiana farm boy who dreamed of the ocean and wanted nothing more than to see the world. She was the ninth child and sixth daughter of Italian American immigrants, living in a busy, noisy household bursting with relatives, food, and shrines to saints and the Virgin Mary. My mother had no desire to go anywhere at all. She loved her small mill town; she loved her small state. But when my father gave her that suitcase, he told her she was going to see the world, with him.

For their honeymoon, they drove 860 miles in an early winter blizzard so that she could meet his relatives in Greensburg, Indiana. To his family, my father was special. He'd left home at seventeen to join the navy; lived in San Francisco, where he had a brief engagement to a Nob Hill debutante;

then was shipped off to China to fight communism. Because of this last assignment, they called him Wong. They didn't know the stories we later heard: how starving people dropped dead right in the street and the sailors were ordered not to help them or they'd have to pay for the funeral. He saw opium dens and brothels and shoot-outs.

His brothers and sisters thought my mother the most exotic bird: dark curly hair, olive skin, a Roman nose, a Catholic who wouldn't eat meat on Friday. Their food—chicken fried in lard, beans cooked with ham hocks, copious amounts of beer—turned her stomach, even though as a young wife she learned to make her husband's favorite dishes. At just nineteen years old, she'd never eaten food at the house of someone who wasn't Italian, and she was frightened and disgusted and only wanted to go home. When she offered to make spaghetti and meatballs for everyone, she couldn't even find garlic in the grocery store. And to my father, *home* was an elusive place, somewhere to stop for gossip and home-cooked meals on your way to other places.

When they first met, my mother fell in love with a tall, blond, blue-eyed sailor in a white dress uniform. She didn't think about how sailors went off to sea, often for long periods of time. She didn't think about how he wouldn't be based in Newport forever, or even for very long. There was always the next base somewhere else, a fact that excited my wanderlust-filled dad and made my mother weary.

He was at sea when their first child was born. My mother,

just turned twenty, married for less than a year, found herself alone in a navy hospital. She still describes that as one of the lowest points in her life—she was scared and ignorant of the ways women gave birth, and my father was so far away. Still, she named my brother after my father, happily adding "Junior" at the end of his name, then promptly nicknamed him Skip, short for Skipper, a nod to his navy father.

After my father returned, with Skip already six months old, he learned that his next post was in Naples, Italy. He thought this would please my mother—her family had come from a small town near Naples fifty years earlier, and many of them still talked with great nostalgia about the old country. But Naples was across a very big ocean from her mother and her sisters, and my mother didn't want to go. So my father went alone. He secured an apartment in the upscale Vomero neighborhood, and wrote love letters telling my mother how he couldn't live without her.

Ultimately she relented, reluctantly. Six months after he left, my father flew home to get her. Surely a part of him worried that if he wasn't there, she might not get on that plane to Naples. The day he arrived, her favorite sister went into the hospital for a routine wisdom tooth extraction. Mom brought her some magazines and promised to go back later, but after six months apart, my young parents were so eager to be alone that they never made it back to the hospital. The next morning, the hospital called: her sister had died from an allergic reaction to the anesthesia.

After the funeral, my father flew back to Naples alone, and a few weeks later my mother left her bereft mother, her sister's widowed husband and two motherless children, and, filled with overwhelming grief, boarded the navy plane with my year-old brother in her arms. She'd never flown before, and everything about the trip terrified her. The plane made frequent unexplained stops, and my mother cried the whole way.

But something happened in Naples. To her surprise, she loved hearing her ancestral tongue spoken, loved the laundry hung across clotheslines suspended between buildings, loved how my brother charmed the vegetable man and the baker and the sausage maker. She taught herself to cook in Naples—ruining pots of beans and overcooking pasta and undercooking meats. But by the time they left, three years later, she was a navy wife, ready to go wherever her husband's next post sent them.

Although she was always homesick, by the time I came along, a year later, my mother was able to pack up our belongings, set up our furniture in new homes, shop the PX, and get us enrolled in school with ease. To me, she was always one of the most competent people I knew. And part of that competence came in the form of what she perfected during those navy years: pies. Beautiful pies. Back at home, her own mother made pies from the fruit she grew in the yard: blueberries, cherries, apples. But my mother's pies were modern, things of beauty. Chocolate cream and lemon meringue. She never made one without the other, and she brought one of each to the potlucks and celebrations the navy families always seemed to be having.

My father's pals and their wives loved my mother's Italian cooking, the meatballs and eggplant Parmesan and veal scaloppine. But it was pie that my mother insisted on making. Looking back, I see now that those pies—so American, so contemporary—represented her own independence, her growing up and away from that big Italian family. Not that she ever stopped missing home or yearning to return but, rather, that out there in the big world my father had promised to show her, she was her own woman.

The lemon meringue remains my favorite. I've tasted lemon meringue pies made with higher, sweeter meringues. Pies made with real lemon curd. But I have never tasted one as good as my mother's. Her topping does not soar but is white and sugary and topped with small browned peaks. (Even now, seeing a pie set on the counter, I steal a peak off the top with my fingers.) Her lemon filling is made from a mix. Her crust is store-bought.

No matter. One taste and I am back in our apartment in Arlington, Virginia, my father at work for Admiral Rickover at the Pentagon. The door opens and he is there in his uniform, and my mother's face lights up as she runs to him and lets him take her into his arms for a movie-star kiss. My brother is eating the chocolate cream pie, I am eating the lemon meringue, and it is so sweet, so sweet, that pie, and this transient life we have together, this family.

GOGO'S LEMON MERINGUE PIE

My mother's name is Gloria Giuianina Masciarotte Hood. When my son, Sam, was young, he called her Grandma Gloria, a nickname his sister Grace tried to say, only it somehow came out Gogo, which stuck. Now everyone—including me—calls her Gogo. Feisty and energetic, even at eighty-six, Gogo's got a nickname that fits.

INGREDIENTS

1 store-bought piecrust (preferably Pillsbury)
1 box Jell-O lemon pudding and pie filling, not instant
4 egg whites
4 tablespoons powdered sugar
1 teaspoon cornstarch
A few drops lemon juice

1. Preheat oven to 350 degrees F.
2. Bake piecrust until lightly browned.
3. Make lemon filling according to package directions. Pour into the browned piecrust.
4. As it cools, make the meringue: combine all remaining ingredients in a bowl and beat with an electric mixer until stiff peaks form.
5. Sprinkle powdered sugar evenly over the top of the filling to keep the meringue from sliding off.

6. Gently pour the meringue onto the pie and bake for three minutes.

7. Let cool out of reach of people who, like me, enjoy eating the browned peaks of meringue.

Variation

Replace the lemon pie filling with chocolate pudding and pie filling—not the instant kind—and the meringue with home-made whipped cream, which you can make by pouring 1 cup of heavy whipping cream into the bowl of a mixer, adding 2 tablespoons of sugar to it, and whipping until soft peaks form. Top the cooled chocolate filling with the whipped cream and you've got yourself a chocolate cream pie. We happen to be a family who likes the skin that forms on the top of pudding, but if you don't, put a piece of plastic wrap over the filling until it cools, at which point you will remove it and then top the pie with the whipped cream.

Gogo's Meatballs

"Teach me," I say to my mother every few years. "Teach me to make meatballs."

She groans and sighs. "There's no *recipe*," she insists.

"I'll just watch you then," I offer, and reluctantly she agrees.

As she combines the ground beef and the eggs and the bread crumbs, mixing it all with her hands, I try to assess what quantity of bread crumbs and how many eggs are going in and to write it down before she adds the garlic and parsley.

The secret to Gogo's meatballs is how you roll them, a skill my father could never master. Neither can I. She demonstrates her technique, which results in firm meatballs that somehow manage to not be too dense. I try, and she shakes her head. "You're like your father," she says sadly. "Soft meatballs."

The first time I made meatballs for my family, I miscalculated the salt. My daughter Grace tasted one and puckered her lips and then spit it out. Sam was more diplomatic. "Interesting," he said, then gently placed the meatball back on his plate.

The next time, my Auntie Junie tasted one and laughed so hard she shot meatball all over herself. "The woman up the street made meatballs like this," she said. "Bad."

Years later, with a now-grown Sam, I went over to Gogo's hoping to have a meatball lesson, but she'd already mixed everything by the time we got there and just needed them rolled.

"I wanted to write down the ingredients," I reminded her. "And the measurements."

"There's no *recipe*," Gogo said again. "Now roll. Like this."

She demonstrated, and Sam and I watched. Then we pinched off the same amount of meatball mixture and began to roll. Gogo's eyes widened with delight. "He can do it," she said, pointing her Carlton 100 at Sam. "Look at how beautiful."

Sam beamed, and placed his perfectly rolled meatballs beside Gogo's.

Without her telling me, I knew: mine were too soft. As if I needed proof, they almost fell apart in the frying pan.

I rolled harder. Once cooked, they sent Auntie Junie into more fits of laughter. "These are like marbles. Remember the woman down the hill? She made meatballs like this."

Gogo's meatballs are best hot, right out of the frying pan, eaten off a fork with no sauce. But they are also good in lots of sauce beside a big bowl of spaghetti. And in grinders, topped with extra sauce and a heavy dusting of Parmesan cheese. Here is the recipe—which, as Gogo says, doesn't really exist. I'm trying to talk Gogo into doing a YouTube video of how to properly roll a meatball. Of course, she refuses. "There's no *recipe*," she says, puffing on her cigarette and proceeding to make the most perfect meatball in the world.

GOGO'S MEATBALLS

Although Gogo insists there's no recipe for her meatballs— or anything else she makes—when pushed, she reluctantly supplies measurements and amounts. However, in our Italian American family, people commonly leave out ingredients or alter recipes in order to ensure that their cookies, bread, egg- plant, or, yes, meatballs are the best in the family. Once my mother was given an almond cookie recipe that deliberately called for too much marzipan, an expensive ingredient that she grumbled about even before the cookies came out wrong. All of this is to say that any recipe I share with you from Gogo is liable to need a little tweaking—more or less salt or garlic or onion. Some of these small errors are because, like all good cooks, Gogo adjusts according to the size of the gar- lic cloves or onions she's using. But be forewarned that she always wants her food to be better than yours.

Makes 13 meatballs

INGREDIENTS

1½ pounds ground beef (don't use lean beef! Gogo suggests 86 percent or lower)

Dusting of salt and pepper

2 eggs

2 to 3 cloves of crushed garlic (depending on size)

¼ cup chopped flat-leaf parsley

Enough bread crumbs to bind everything together; start with ¼ cup and increase as needed (if you make your own, use white bread; if you use store-bought—which Gogo usually does—make sure they are plain, not seasoned)

1. Put everything except the bread crumbs into a big bowl.
2. Mix it up with your hands. (Mama Rose, my grandmother, gave this task to the grandchildren; there are few joys greater than playing with food.)
3. Add the bread crumbs about ¼ cup at a time, mixing each addition in and stopping when the mixture binds together. (It is very important not to use too much.)
4. Roll the mixture into meatballs. To determine how big each ball should be, remember that you should have thirteen meatballs for every 1½ pounds of meat.

NOTE: According to Gogo, the rolling is the most important part of making meatballs. Take enough meat mixture in your palm to make one meatball. Keep that hand still, and roll with the palm of your other hand until you feel the mixture growing into a round ball.

5. Place the formed meatballs on a plate.
6. Pour enough canola oil to reach about halfway up a meatball into a frying pan and heat on high. When it starts to sizzle and a small pinch of meat mixture tossed in fries right up, reduce the heat to medium.
7. Lower the meatballs into the oil and fry until the bottoms are browned. ("How long is that, Gogo?" "Until they're brown!") Then flip and fry the other half until brown.

A NOTE ON GOGO'S MEATBALLS: They are not soft on the outside, so be sure they are browned nicely.

8. The meatballs might still be a little pink on the inside. This is all right because you will put them in the red sauce while it simmers to finish cooking them. However, leave several in the frying pan a bit longer to get rid of the pink if you want to stick them on forks and eat them hot, without sauce, as a snack.
9. Save the frying oil in a coffee can for reasons to be revealed in "Gogo's Sauce" (page 151).

Love, Lunch, and
Meatball Grinders

When I was in elementary school, we began our day by wishing the teacher good morning, followed by the Pledge of Allegiance and an off-key rendition of a patriotic song, which is to say this was the 1960s, when kids still hid under their desks to practice what to do when the atom bomb fell. The Providence Street Grammar School was built in 1914. One classroom for each grade, as many as forty kids in a class. The wood floors were polished and shiny, the chalk yellow, the chalkboard green. We did our work—and ate our lunches—at our old wooden desks.

Every night after supper, my mother made lunches for my brother and me. She used brown paper bags, the same kind we cut into book covers for our textbooks. By day, my Italian American mother worked in a candy factory while my father kept America safe, stationed in Cuba with the navy.

I've come to believe those school lunches were my mother's only creative outlet. She didn't have time to knit or sew—unless a button fell off our winter coats—or read. But she threw everything into those lunches. All of her energy and culinary desires, and all of the food in the house. Fried chicken—two pieces—bread and butter, Fritos, a Devil Dog, and half a pound of cherries; a meatball grinder wet with spaghetti sauce, two apples, and a mini blueberry pie. You get the idea.

These things were so enormous that I had to carry them not by the rolled-up top of the bag but like another geography book, large and heavy and unwieldy. I envied the kids walking down the street while jauntily swinging their metal *Jetsons* lunch boxes. The kids who opened those lunch boxes and pulled from them a fluffernutter on white bread, an Oreo or two, and a small apple.

One girl had the most magical sandwich of all: one side white bread, the other side something called wheat bread, with a light smear of Miracle Whip and a thin slice of ham. That sandwich was so delicate, so lovely, that it caused the first pangs of jealousy I ever felt. One day I screwed up enough courage to ask her if she'd like to trade. I spread my haul across the desktop.

"What've you got?" she asked, narrowing her eyes and bending her head, with its pixie haircut, to survey it.

What did I have? Everything!

But she only wrinkled her nose, turned her head, and took

a delicate bite of her exotic sandwich, leaving me to gnaw on chicken and hide cherry pits in my desk.

When I had children of my own, I made them thin cucumber slices, turkey and cheese rolled and cut into delicate pinwheels, airy meringues. One day at pickup, Sam's kindergarten teacher grabbed my arm. "Sam's lunches," she began, and I beamed with pride. My kid had the perfect school lunches, and I knew it. "They're measly!" she announced. "He needs more food. He's asking everyone to share theirs with him. He's *hungry*." I wish I could say I changed my ways. But my youngest, Annabelle, still suffers from my desire to re-create the lunches I longed for. I remove her crusts and use cookie cutters to make her sandwiches into hearts and stars. I husk strawberries. And as I do, I remember my own brown bags groaning with food.

Growing up as an awkward bookworm in a house crammed with so many people, with a mother who worked and came home tired each night, I often felt lonely. Of course Mom and I went on shopping sprees at the mall and for lunches at local restaurants. But mostly she was vacuuming or ironing or gabbing with her sisters around the kitchen table, playing backgammon with my father, or taking a well-deserved nap. I wasn't as funny or outrageous as my brother, who garnered attention like a comet streaking across the kitchen.

My mother built lunches the way some people build skyscrapers or monuments. It wasn't until I was an adult that I realized they were her Taj Mahal—all of that glorious food jammed into a brown paper bag, made only for me.

GOGO'S MEATBALL GRINDERS

In Rhode Island, we call milkshakes *cabinets*, water fountains *bubblers*, and subs or hoagies *grinders*. To make Gogo's Meatball Grinders, think big and think messy. These are not for lightweights. Of course, you can use fewer meatballs and less sauce, but please don't tell Gogo.

INGREDIENTS

16 ounces or more of your favorite red sauce (page 151), warm
13 meatballs, or one batch of Gogo's Meatballs (page 30),
   warmed in red sauce
Enough Parmesan cheese for heavy sprinkling
Enough shredded mozzarella for melting on top (optional)
3 or 4 hard grinder rolls, big enough to hold 4 meatballs
   (interpret as you like, using your favorite type)

1. Split the tops of the rolls.
2. Spread a good amount of sauce on both sides. Don't be prudent here!
3. Although you probably have had meatball grinders in which the meatballs are cut in half, we use them whole. So line them up in the roll. They should be saucy from sitting in the warm sauce, but you also want to add more sauce once they're in the roll.
4. Sprinkle a good amount of Parmesan cheese on top.

5. Grab lots of napkins.

6. Eat.

Optional

Top with shredded mozzarella and stick under the broiler until the mozzarella is melted and the roll is toasted. Keep an eye on it because this happens fast, usually in under a minute. Then go to steps 5 and 6.

Fancy Food

When I was a kid, I thought my mother was the fanciest woman around. She wore a wiglet, a small clip-on piece of synthetic auburn hair that gave her the much-desired added pouf that stylish women in 1965 placed on top of their heads. Before every holiday, she redecorated our house, turning it into a theme park of hearts and cupids, leprechauns and shamrocks, Easter bunnies and colorful eggs, red, white, and blue everything, turkeys and ghosts and snowmen. Even our bathroom got a makeover, with the shower curtain and bath mat changing from red to green to yellow to navy blue to orange and brown. My mother wore a red matte lipstick that ringed the cigarette butts she left in the heavy harvest gold ashtray by her favorite chair in the living room. Unlike the heavy, dark, plastic-covered furniture my aunts had in their houses, thanks to my mother we had Danish contemporary:

a pink armchair, a low turquoise sofa, and an orange vinyl bucket chair that spun around. Fancy.

But it wasn't just what she wore or how she fixed up our house; it was the food she made that convinced me of her sophistication. She imitated the women she saw in glossy magazines to escape her Italian American, blue-collar roots—an impossible feat really, since we lived with her mother and grandmother and other assorted relatives, all of them with one foot back in the old country. My mother bought grapefruit spoons, small teaspoons with serrated edges for removing the wedges of pink grapefruit she served in fancy glass bowls. We were Catholic, which meant no meat on Fridays. Most Fridays, Mama Rose served up polenta with kale or Eggs in Purgatory (sunny-side-up eggs in red sauce) or pasta fagioli. But every now and then, my mother would take over the kitchen. She'd make a simple white sauce, add canned tuna and canned peas and carrots to it, and serve it on toast points—small triangles of white bread that she'd carefully cut and remove the crusts from. I hated that cream of tuna. It smelled like cat food and tasted even worse. But I admired its beauty: the toast triangles and glossy white sauce and bright bits of green and orange.

The fanciest food my mother made were her salads—ham and chicken. Usually they appeared in finger rolls on large silver trays for bridal showers, card games, or PTA meetings. Sometimes they showed up for lunch on a Saturday afternoon, elegant and exotic, nestled close together on one of those trays. Mom put the meat through an old-fashioned meat grinder, rendering it almost smooth, without any traces of fat or gristle. To each salad she added mayonnaise, only Hellmann's. Then the chicken salad got celery and onion, both diced so small that they were indiscernible except for the crunch and flavor they provided. To the ham salad she added diced sweet gherkins and nothing more. The result was two distinct flavors, and it was impossible for me to choose a favorite. My mother, presiding over a tray of those sandwiches in her red lipstick and wiglet, seemed fancier to me than her favorite movie star, Sophia Loren.

When I was in fourth grade, my mother volunteered as a PTA parent for my school. She had always been a relentless champion for my older brother and his activities—a Cub Scout den mother and junior high dance chaperone on Friday nights. But this was her first time volunteering at my school, and as the night for the big fall PTA meeting drew near, my pride and excitement grew. In class we decorated the room with cornucopias we'd traced and cut out, then glued fruit we'd colored onto them so it appeared the fruit was spilling out. That Sunday, Mom took out the meat grinder and produced mounds of ham and chicken for her salads. Instead of the usual finger rolls, she went to a bakery and bought bread that had been dyed neon blue, pink, and green. She rolled the bread out thin and cut it into the shapes of daisies and circles and diamonds, dropped heaping tablespoons of chicken and ham salad onto each one and topped it with a matching shape. The result was a dizzyingly beautiful array of brightly colored tea sandwiches, so stunning that I begged her to leave some behind. Instead, she'd counted how many people were attending the meeting and multiplied that by the amount of sandwiches they would each eat and made the exact right number.

My father was recruited to carry the trays to the car and from there into the school, where he would wait for the meeting to end and then take the empty trays and my mother back home. Off they went, Mom dressed in camel and fake fur, Dad in his glen-plaid suit and wingtips. I stood at the door, glowing with pride over my beautiful mother and her fancy sandwiches. The PTA meeting would begin at six, but my parents drove away in their green Chevy just before five, so that they would arrive with plenty of time to set up. Despite the time, it was already dark out, and as I watched the taillights disappear around the corner I imagined my teacher's face when she saw those sandwiches. I was an unpopular kid. My classmates whispered insults to me under their breath or called me names on the playground, leaving me unchosen for games of kickball. I spent hours alone, playing jacks on the asphalt. I imagined that all this would be somehow erased when their parents reported that my mother had created the most sophisticated food they'd ever eaten.

With the meeting and then the cleanup afterward, my parents weren't expected home until eight or nine. Thursdays offered some of my favorite TV shows—*Shindig* and *The Munsters* and *Batman*—and I was already sitting in front of the television when the lights flickered and then went out. Everything went out—stove, lights, television. Mama Rose screamed and moaned and wept. "It's the Russians!" she wailed. "They're coming for us!" From a distance of over fifty years, this seems both reasonable and probable for 1965. While she lit candles and said prayers in Italian, I hid under the kitchen table— ducking and covering like they taught us to do at school.

Then: the sound of car doors slamming.

I peeked out from beneath my hiding spot and saw Mama Rose, eerie in the candlelight, hurrying to the front door. Terrified, I followed, holding tight to her apron. The street-lights were out, too. In fact, our entire neighborhood was absolutely dark, except for the small interior light of my parents' Chevy, which illuminated them: my mother pale and anxious, my father sliding the full tray of sandwiches from the back seat.

"The whole town lost electricity," my father said when he saw us standing outside the door.

"What about the PTA meeting?" I cried.

My mother got out of the car, and when she slammed her door shut, only the glowing tip of her cigarette lit the darkness.

"Canceled," she said. "And me stuck with all these fucking sandwiches."

THE FIRST TIME I made a grown-up lunch, I was twenty-four years old and living alone in a little apartment by the sea. A college friend was passing through town, and I invited her over. As soon as she accepted, I went into a panic. What did someone make a guest for lunch? When I went out for lunch, I tended toward club sandwiches and French dip, neither of which seemed like the thing to serve an old friend. I stared into my refrigerator at the previous night's leftover chicken, breast meat still clinging to its bones. In that moment, I realized that all those chicken salad and ham salad sandwiches my mother had made weren't because she was so fancy; for a Depression-era daughter of immigrants, they came from frugality. Nothing gets wasted or thrown away. Add some mayo or celery or sweet gherkins to leftover ham and chicken and you have a whole new dish, unrecognizable from the roast chicken and mashed potato dinner or the ham studded with cloves and pineapple rings.

I rummaged through my box of recipes clipped from magazines and newspapers and found one from *Glamour* magazine for curried chicken salad. This was in 1982, long enough ago that I couldn't find that same recipe when I searched the Internet recently. It's vanished, along with the shoulder pads and feathered bangs we all wore back then. I remember grapes, walnuts, raisins, and curry, of course. When my friend arrived, I presented her with a scoop of curried chicken salad sitting on top of lettuce (iceberg, no doubt, since that was lettuce to me back then). This friend, also named Ann, had grown up in New York City going to museums and concerts. She was at that time the most sophisticated person of my age that I knew.

She looked at that lunch, the shredded lettuce and golden chicken salad, and she said, "Hood! This is so fancy! Look at you!"

Something swelled up inside me: a new, deeper understanding of my mother. I saw her at our kitchen table (topped with a thematic tablecloth: happy snowmen or grinning jack-o'-lanterns) with that old-fashioned meat grinder, making the fanciest food I'd ever been served.

FANCY-LADY SANDWICHES

In an essay from *Dimestore: A Writer's Life*, Lee Smith writes about her mother's battered recipe box, which her mother "antiqued" by decoupaging kitchen-themed decals onto it—a skillet, a rolling pin, a milk bottle. In it are recipes for funerals and for southern specialties like pimento cheese; sixteen recipes for oysters; clams "every whichaway"; fancy recipes for Lady Baltimore Cake and Soiree Punch. But the description I like best of all is of her mama's noon bridge club, which met every Thursday until its members moved to Florida or began to die off. Smith describes her mother's polka-dot dress, the cut flowers and pink cloths on the table. Lunch for the bridge club was a molded Jell-O salad, Chicken Crunch, and Lime Angel Cloud. (Please please please read this book, and everything else by Lee Smith, if you haven't already.) My mother did not have a bridge club. She had a Friday night penny poker club, all of the women toting coffee cans over-flowing with pennies.

When it was my mother's turn to host her poker club, I sat on the stairs and watched the ladies arrive. My mother laid out her finger sandwiches on a silver tray, and they looked so fancy that no one would ever guess they were made from leftovers. There are only two of the original thirteen ladies left, and due to physical limitations and old age, they don't meet up anymore. But Gogo still talks with bittersweet nos-talgia about Auntie Dora's torpedo fill sandwiches (kind of a Sloppy Joe with more spice), Jackie's stuffed artichokes, Carmela's crescent rolls stuffed with water chestnut and beef. Me? I like the fancy-lady sandwiches.

GOGO'S CHICKEN SALAD

Gogo's chicken and ham salads rely on common sense. The amount of meat to mayo and add-ins varies. As Gogo would say: "Go slow and figure it out."

INGREDIENTS

Leftover chicken, white meat only, ground fine (Gogo used an old-fashioned meat grinder that attached to the edge of the kitchen table and was cranked, but you can use a food processor)

½ onion (more if you have a lot of leftover chicken), diced fine

A couple stalks of celery, diced fine
Salt and pepper
Enough mayo to moisten and bind
Finger rolls

1. Grind everything separately. First the chicken, then remove it and put it in a bowl; then the onion, and add it to the chicken; then the celery, and add it to the chicken and onion.
2. Add salt and pepper to taste.
3. Spoon in mayo by the heaping tablespoon, mixing after each addition until you reach the consistency you like.
4. Make finger sandwiches.
5. Serve on a fancy tray.

GOGO'S HAM SALAD

INGREDIENTS

Leftover ham, finely ground in a food processor
4 to 6 sweet gherkins (depending on how much ham you have and how big the pickles are)
Salt and pepper
Enough mayo to moisten and bind
Finger rolls

1. Grind the ham and the sweet gherkins separately.
2. Combine together in a bowl.

3. Sprinkle with salt and pepper.
4. Spoon in mayo by the heaping tablespoon, mixing after each addition until you reach the consistency you like.
5. Make finger sandwiches.
6. Serve on a silver tray.

GLAMOUROUS CURRIED CHICKEN SALAD

That curried chicken salad recipe I clipped from a long-ago *Glamour* magazine and made for lunch for my friend Ann disappeared decades ago. But I still love making and eating curried chicken salad. It is one of my son Sam's favorite things, especially when I top it with salted cashews.

Serves 6 very hungry people or 8 who are moderately hungry

INGREDIENTS

1½ pounds cooked chicken breasts (I often buy the rotisserie
ones from the grocery store)
½ cup mayo
A couple of stalks of celery, diced
5 teaspoons (or more, to taste) of good curry powder
A handful of golden raisins

Optional
The above makes a delicious curried chicken salad, even more so if you prepare it the day before you eat it, so the

flavors mingle together. But below are optional ingredients that you can add if you have them on hand. I am not a big fan of raw onions, so I leave them out. However, I've been known to throw in some scallions if I have a few lying around. The chutney adds a nice depth to the salad, but I usually add it only if I plan ahead and remember to buy it.

1 diced apple
¼ cup Major Grey's chutney, or your favorite type
½ diced red onion or 2 to 3 chopped scallions
½ cup cashews, salted, chopped or whole or ½ cup dry-roasted
*   peanuts*

1. Chop the chicken breasts into bite-sized pieces
2. Add the rest of the ingredients, including the apple, chutney, onion, or scallions if you are using, and mix up well.
3. Serve in pita bread, on a bed of lettuce, or in finger rolls.

CHICKEN SALAD VERONIQUE

I fell in love with tarragon in the 1980s when a Silver Palate recipe called for it. Of course, back then I used the dried stuff, but eventually I found fresh tarragon, and it is truly my favorite herb. For something with such a fancy French name, Chicken Salad Veronique is actually very simple to make: it's a basic chicken salad with grapes and tarragon. Once I had it with pecans in it, and another time with slivered almonds. You are, of course, free to add either, but I'm a purist. As Pierre Franey wrote about the Burgundy dish Chicken Veronique in the *New York Times* in 1978, "Among the foods best suited to a hasty meal are those that are skinless and boneless and tender besides." Franey's classic recipe uses a cream sauce with shallots, white wine, and grapes; "Veronique" denotes a chicken (or fish) dish made with grapes.

Serves 4 for lunch or a midnight snack

INGREDIENTS

1½ cups cooked and chopped boneless, skinless chicken breasts
½ cup mayo
1½ tablespoons chopped fresh tarragon
1 or 2 stalks celery, diced
1 cup white or red seedless grapes, halved
½ cup slivered almonds or chopped pecans if you're not a purist like me
Salt and pepper to taste

1. Mix all the ingredients together.
2. Serve on a bed of lettuce, on your favorite bread for a sandwich, or in finger rolls.

Confessions of a Marsha Jordan Girl

When blueberries are in season and I am feeling nostalgic for my younger days, I dig out a purple-stained recipe from my recipe box and begin to bake blueberry muffins. Although the ingredients—butter, flour, sugar, vanilla, eggs, baking powder, milk, and salt—do not seem magical, combined in a certain way with enough blueberries to turn the batter a pale purple and topped with a heavy sprinkling of sugar, these muffins transport me back in time.

As they bake, if I close my eyes, I can go back to when I was Ann-Marie, not Ann. I can picture a happy half dozen muffins snuggled into a white bakery box, the lid open and me trying to choose the blueberriest one of them all. It is a long-ago Sunday afternoon and our house is filled with relatives, some who show up every Sunday and some who drift in and out over the years. My Italian grandmother, Mama Rose, is hoisting a pan of lasagna from the oven, trimming fennel to serve with a dish of oil for dipping, stirring a pot of red sauce—*gravy,* we called it—and making coffee seemingly all at the same time, moving around our tiny kitchen—*the pantry*—as if she's in a well-choreographed ballet. That coffee was made right on the stove, with eggshells added to the grounds to cut the bitterness. In the kitchen—the room other people would have called the dining room—the relatives ate Auntie Etta's small, round cookies fried and covered in honey, then topped with colored sprinkles; delicate butter cookies shaped like wreaths and seashells; and her daffodil cake, an angel food cake with egg yolks stirred in at the right time to create the shape of daffodils in bloom.

The muffins came from the Jordan Marsh Bakery, all the way in Boston. I had never been to Boston, never been to Jordan Marsh. It loomed large and sparkling in my imagination. I imagined it looked like a palace, its floors filled with dazzling mirrors and fancy women spritzing perfume at customers as they passed. We had department stores in Rhode Island, sure. But none that produced muffins the size of tennis balls.

The only competition for Jordan Marsh was its rival store, Filene's. My birthday, December 9, came the day before my godmother's birthday. Auntie Ellen was a romantic heroine. Tall and blond, with her makeup always perfect and her hair always flipped just so, she had no children of her own, and this gave her an air of tragedy but also added to her mystery. Auntie Ellen never had to run off to pick up anyone, never smelled of applesauce or baby like the other aunts, who were all mothers. Unlike them, she had the time to go all the way to Boston to shop at Filene's. She bought my birthday presents there, delivering them in their store wrapping paper and tied with a perfect red bow. One year, I opened the box to find a brown suede bracelet with a gold rectangle in the center. In that rectangle, in the fanciest script I had ever seen, my own name: Ann-Marie.

WILLIAM FILENE, a German immigrant, founded Filene's, which was originally called Filene's Sons and Company and encompassed a group of many small shops. In 1881 Filene combined them to create his department store on Washington Street, where, twenty years earlier, Eben Dyer Jordan and Benjamin L. Marsh had opened Jordan Marsh and Company, the first "departmentalized" store in the country.

Filene's and Jordan Marsh began many of the services contemporary shoppers take for granted. Both stores were elegantly designed, with products from around the world sold in different departments. Edward Filene, William's son, opened the bargain annex that came to be known as the famous Filene's Basement. He also developed an automatic markdown schedule to discount merchandise that is still used today. Filene's slogan was "Money back if not satisfied." Next door, Jordan Marsh pioneered its own services for shoppers, including charge accounts and the policy that the customer is always right. It was also one of the first stores to feature electric lights, glass showcases, telephones, and elevators. And it had art galleries, a bakery that produced those fancy blueberry muffins, and fashion shows, a specialty that eventually reached across almost a century to me in Warwick, Rhode Island.

THE WARWICK MALL opened about two miles from my house in 1970, when I was thirteen years old. At one end: Filene's. At the other: Jordan Marsh. The arrival of these two department stores heralded an opportunity to buy the clothes and makeup I drooled over every month in *Seventeen* magazine. It meant that even for a girl like me, someone who sat and stared out the window dreaming of a vague but glamourous future, sophistication was within my grasp. The stores were exactly as I'd hoped. They dazzled and enchanted me with their displays of goods. Cosmetic counters filled the entire first floor, and the air smelled of Chanel and Shalimar. When I walked into either department store, I became someone new. They held the future, I thought. *My* future.

One afternoon as I stepped into Jordan Marsh from the mall entrance, a woman called to me. She had the best posture I'd ever seen, and she sat at a makeshift desk. Her smile stretched brightly across her face.

"Have you ever considered modeling?" she asked me.

"Yes," I said without hesitating. I had considered every occupation I thought would throw me headfirst into a glamourous life: model, cruise ship hostess, airline stewardess.

"We're putting together a fashion board of eight girls," she explained. "Marsha Jordan girls," she added.

Before she could continue, I was filling out the application.

"Do you know what you're going to wear on the first day of school?" she asked me.

Know? I had made a chart of my outfits all the way through October.

"Hot-pink hot pants with a matching maxi vest and a pink flowered shirt," I said.

"Hot pants with a maxi vest?" she repeated, impressed. She made a note and told me that sixteen girls would be called for final interviews.

By the time I got home that afternoon, Jordan Marsh had called. I was one of the sixteen finalists. In an afternoon, I had gone from a regular girl with oversized dreams to an almost Marsha Jordan girl. A week later, I was in the upper-floor conference room of the store, eating brownie sundaes with executives and answering questions about everything from what makeup I liked—*Bonne Belle!*—to my favorite novel—*Marjorie Morningstar!* Every Jordan Marsh store in New England had Marsha Jordan girls, high school girls who were models in fashion shows in the stores and at mother-daughter teas, who did tests and surveys about fashion in the malls and in their schools, whose pictures hung on spinning cubes in the junior clothing department. By the time I left that interview, I knew I had to be a Marsha Jordan girl. I *had* to.

I was told they'd call by five-thirty. But five-thirty came and went and no one called. At six, I was hysterical, begging Mama Rose to pray to Saint Anthony, her patron saint. Puzzled by what exactly to pray for, she nonetheless set to work in front of his statue in our living room. My mother ordered me outside; I was making her nervous. When the phone rang at six-fifteen, I was too nervous to answer. But my father did. I heard his slow greeting and then: "Ann," he said, "it's someone from Jordan Marsh calling for you." I grabbed that phone from his hand and said hello to my future.

THE SEVEN OTHER Marsha Jordan girls and I were given uniforms, gray-and-white striped pants and jacket, a cranberry blouse with white cuffs and collar. We traveled on our own by bus to that flagship store on Washington Street for fittings and fashion shows. We ate chicken divan crepes at the Magic Pan and salads with sticky buns at the English Tea Room on Newbury Street. We hailed cabs and walked across the Boston Common, a gaggle of long-haired, long-legged sixteen-year-olds. At home, we stood on pedestals, mannequin modeling. We dated college boys who worked at the store for their summer jobs, getting first kisses in their Fiats and Mustangs in the parking lot. On one night in December, the store closed for Men's Night, and only men were allowed to come in; they shopped for their wives and girlfriends while we walked around the store in a revolving array of clothes. Bonne Bell sent us makeup to try, and cartons of Ten-O-Six lotion to tackle our pimples.

I wanted my days as a Marsha Jordan girl, with those summers of long kisses with boys and hours of fittings and runway shows, to go on and on. But like all things, those days eventually did end, and soon I was off to college, where I traded in that gray-and-white pin-striped uniform for one of khaki pants and an Izod shirt. I still went to Filene's and Jordan Marsh when I wanted to buy something special— Christmas gifts for my mom, beautiful housewares as friends got married, splurges for myself. And then I traded in my preppy uniform for the Ralph Lauren–designed TWA flight attendant uniform. On layovers I rode the escalators in department stores in Paris and London, San Francisco and Manhattan. Harrods was bigger, Bendel's more chic, Nordstrom grander. But none of them compared to my first loves, those early visions of glamour and sophistication that anchored the Warwick Mall back home.

Filene's and Jordan Marsh are gone now. At the mall, Macy's and Target have taken their places. Like my childhood dreams, they have faded in my memory. But when I bake those muffins from a recipe straight from the Jordan Marsh Bakery, when I pull them from the over warm and sparkling with sugar, I can almost go back there. I close my eyes and take a bite, and a rush of images passes through me. My mother in Filene's, testing a new shade of red lipstick. My friends and me buying 45s of Three Dog Night and Simon and Garfunkel in the Jordan Marsh record department. I am giggling with my friend Beth. I am opening a slender box and finding a brown suede bracelet with my name engraved on a gold plate: Ann-Marie. The muffins are sweet. Their taste lingers for a long moment before it is gone.

JORDAN MARSH BLUEBERRY MUFFINS

If you were lucky enough to visit a Jordan Marsh Bakery, you know that these muffins were huge and sweet—the tops were covered in sugar. You can find recipes for them in the *New York Times* and other venerable newspapers and food magazines. But the one I use came straight from a Jordan Marsh baker, John Pupek, in an interview he gave to Boston's WCVB anchor Maria Stephanos. When she asked Pupek if he liked making the legendary muffins, he replied, "It was my life." Here is his recipe:

Makes 12 muffins

INGREDIENTS

   ½ cup butter
   1 cup sugar, plus 2 teaspoons for the muffins' tops
   2 eggs
   2 cups flour (unsifted, an equal blend of bread and pastry)
   2 teaspoons baking powder
   ½ cup milk
   2½ cups blueberries
   1 teaspoon vanilla

1. Preheat the oven to 375 degrees F.
2. On low speed, cream the butter with the sugar until it's fluffy.

3. Add the eggs one at a time and mix until blended.

4. Sift the dry ingredients; add to the eggs-and-butter mixture, alternating with the milk.

5. Mash ½ cup of the berries and stir into the mixture by hand.

6. Add the rest of the berries whole and stir by hand.

7. Grease a muffin tin well with butter; grease the top surface of the pans as well. (No offense to Mr. Pupek, but I use muffin liners instead, preferably with funny designs on them.)

8. Pile the mixture high in each muffin cup, and sprinkle the sugar over their tops.

9. Bake for 30 minutes.

My Father's Pantry

My father fed me. Shake 'n Bake pork chops, Rice-A-Roni. Always together and always gummy, with a side of canned peas swimming in margarine. Meatloaf mixed with dried onion soup served with so much ketchup I don't remember how it tasted. He wrapped chicken, canned potatoes, cream of mushroom soup, and a hefty dose of poultry seasoning in tinfoil, cooked it on the grill, and called it Chicken Bountiful. I stayed thirsty for a week after eating it. When he made me a grilled cheese sandwich, he pressed it so flat I could have used it as a Frisbee. He burned it on one side; the other side was hardly cooked at all. He served that grilled cheese with Campbell's tomato soup made with milk instead of water and spiked with lots of celery salt. He put sugar in scrambled eggs, salt on watermelon, and orange American cheese on apple pie. I did the same. Not because it tasted good, but because I liked the oddity of it. "Pass the salt," I'd say when I grabbed a slice of watermelon. My father would nod. "That's right. Watermelon has no flavor without salt." When he made mac and cheese, he used that same orange American cheese, a basic white sauce, elbow macaroni, his beloved celery salt, and dried mustard. He called it Baked Macaroni. It was his specialty. Celery salt was his favorite spice, his secret ingredient.

All to say, my father was not a good cook.

But he thought he was. He would say, "You like that fancy coffee, huh? Me, I like Colombian." Then he would show me a brand-new can of Maxwell House. This was not intended as a joke.

He believed that eating chestnuts and mangoes could be fatal.

The fuzz on a peach could send him running in circles, screaming.

After he baked a ham with ginger ale, canned pineapple, and maraschino cherries, he put the ham bone in a big pot of water with dried navy beans and simmered it all day. This dish actually tasted good. I used to sop the broth up with Italian bread while my father hovered around me, beaming.

My father's packaged cakes fell, his piecrusts burned, his roasts were too dry, his pancakes too wet.

But he fed me and fed me and fed me. And I opened my mouth and ate.

IMAGINE A six-foot-three midwesterner dressed in a U.S. Navy uniform landing in an Italian American family in a mill town in the middle of Rhode Island. Blond-haired and blue-eyed, with the long, lazy vowels of southern Indiana, my father had been raised on lard: the chicken was fried in it, the piecrust was made from it, the frosting was whipped with it.

My mother did not know how to cook then. She didn't need to. Her mother did it for the entire family. Not just our family of four, but any of her ten children and their families who happened by looking for meatballs or pigs in a blanket or a plate of lasagna. When we finally moved away from Mama Rose and Rhode Island, my mother tried her hand at domesticity. This was 1960. She wanted to shed her Italian heritage and reinvent herself as an American Wife and Mother. That meant hamburgers and hot dogs, lemon meringue pie, Toll House cookies.

She smoked her cigarettes out of a black cigarette holder, vacuumed in a dress with a full skirt and heels, lined up Drambuie and Dubonnet along a shelf. When my father came home from his job at the Pentagon, she mixed him a martini while he watched *The Huntley-Brinkley Report* from our contemporary Danish turquoise sofa.

This arrangement lasted for three years. Then my father got stationed in Cuba, and my mother packed us up and moved us back to Mama Rose's house, where she took off her apron and went to work in one of the local mills. Mama Rose fed us for the next dozen years, until I was nineteen—right up until the day she made thirty-six meatballs and a gallon of red sauce, sat down in a chair, and died.

■ ■ ■

MY FATHER BEGAN to cook for me when he returned from Cuba, and my mother was happily working. Every Wednesday night, my older brother, Skip, went to his junior high social. He dabbed on my father's Old Spice and slicked his hair back with Vitalis, put on a tie, and got in our family's green Chevrolet Caprice. My mother went along to chaperone.

As soon as they disappeared from our street, my father and I took out my Easy-Bake oven. Into miniature cupcake tins and cake pans we poured mixes that only required adding water. I would peer into the oven as the light bulb inside it glowed. Finally, a ding announced that our cake or brownies were done, my father took the pan out, poured us each a glass of milk, and the two of us sat together and ate. It was awful, of course. Powdery and chemical-tasting, everything either too dry or too moist. But every Wednesday night for three years, my father and I baked.

By the time I reached eighth grade, Skip had left for college. When my mother went to play poker with her girlfriends on Friday nights, my father took me to a place called Freddie's for pizza. While we ate, he told me about growing up in a small town in Indiana during the Depression, how they were so poor that all he got for Christmas was oranges. Once, unable to pay for oranges, his mother made him a doll out of rags. He told me about running away from home and getting a tattoo when he was fourteen and running away again and joining the navy when he was seventeen. In China he ate hundred-year-old eggs, and in Morocco he ate dog stuffed with rice. "It all tasted good to me," he'd say, draining his Michelob. "Maybe that's why I like to cook so much."

He did like to. He just couldn't get it quite right.

He retired early and took over Mama Rose's job as family cook. Every morning, he sat at the kitchen table with a yellow pad and pencil, *The Fannie Farmer Cookbook* open in front of him. From it, he designed menus. Often, he spent the entire rest of the day cooking. But his pork roast came out too pink, his mashed potatoes too runny. My mother might complain or give him cooking tips, but she was glad to have someone else doing it, and didn't want him to quit.

As for me, when he handed me a plate of overcooked pasta, grinning with pride, what could I do except take it and eat? "Mmmmm," I'd say. "How did you make this?"

"Well, I took a bag of frozen mixed vegetables . . ." he'd begin.

WHEN I MOVED to New York City, I entered a world of beef vindaloo, sashimi, pork buns, and risotto. On visits home, I'd still compliment my father on his mushy meatballs or lopsided red velvet cake. But I couldn't help describing the truly good food I now ate regularly. I would take him to my favorite restaurants when he visited me. He'd marvel at the spit-roasted lamb and the Szechuan beef. "Maybe I should get a Chinese cookbook," he'd say as he examined his strangely flavored chicken. "I could probably make this at home. No problem."

Slowly, surprisingly, I began to long for my father's cooking. Alone in my tiny apartment on Bleecker Street, I would
find myself thinking about my father's overcooked roasts
or his sweet scrambled eggs. He always whistled while he
cooked. With the city sounds coming through my window,
my stomach full of tandoori chicken and samosas, I missed
that sound, those tastes from my childhood. Over time, I
came to realize that it wasn't really his cooking that I yearned
for but my father himself. He always set the table just so, his
food placed on fancy Italian platters decorated with roosters or
fruit. He fussed and tweaked, stood back to survey the meal,
then fussed some more, until finally he would sit across from
me and we would begin to eat and talk. His food was only the
prop for his stories, the entrance to our father-daughter talks.
Once, when I got my heart broken, I jumped on the Amtrak
train to Providence. My father waited for me at home, a big
pan of baked mac and cheese in the oven, the American cheese
clinging to the macaroni. When I was sick with pneumonia
and alone in my tiny apartment, my father drove the nearly
two hundred miles to Manhattan and cooked for me: his thick
beef Stroganoff, his dry pork chops. I coughed and burned
with fever and my father kept feeding me until I got better.

Eventually, I moved back to Rhode Island, got married, had
children. When I was pregnant with my first baby, the midwife thought I wasn't gaining enough weight. By the time I got
home from her office, my father was at my doorstep with dozens of cartons of Ben & Jerry's ice cream. After my amniocen-
tesis, during my second pregnancy, I had to stay in bed for the

day, and he showed up with a roast chicken. "I stick an apple up its butt," he said proudly as I peered inside. "That's why it's so moist." It wasn't, of course. Everything he put in the oven, he overcooked. But I devoured that chicken, and the canned peas and scalloped potatoes made from a box and the bottled gravy he served with it. My father sat on the bed with me while I ate, grinning and nodding. "That's my girl," he said.

The day I went into labor with that second baby, the midwife sent me home after she examined me and ordered me to eat a good lunch. Before long, my father was in my kitchen with a pot of beef stew. Beef stew was actually one of his more successful dishes. He carefully trimmed the beef himself and used tomato sauce for the broth. The canned potatoes and carrots lost most of their metallic taste after the stew had simmered all morning. That September day, my father and I sat in my big kitchen with rain splashing the windows, and he filled my bowl with stew. "I will never forget the day you were born," he told me, marveling at how well I was handling my labor. "It was the happiest day of my life."

I held out my bowl for more.

A WEEK AFTER my daughter Grace was born, my father was diagnosed with inoperable lung cancer. By winter, he was bald and weak from chemo and in and out of the hospital with pneumonia and infections. In February, he entered for the final time and stayed for two months. At first, he was lucid and hungry, despite the tubes pumping oxygen into his nose and the mask over his mouth providing still more oxygen. He asked me to bring him Chinese food and ribs from our favorite rib joint.

Soon, though, his appetite began to wane. Every morning, I dressed Grace in pretty dresses with matching hats and stopped at my father's favorite bakery for Danish pastry. He took the white cardboard box from me happily. When he opened it, he'd say, "Oh! You got blueberry, my favorite." But the Danish remained uneaten, nestled in the box. He would take Grace from me, too, and hold her for as long as he could. "You were the most beautiful baby I ever saw," he said to me. "Until I saw Gracie."

The hospital bed had a scale built into it. Every day I watched my father's weight drop. Desperate to keep him alive, I invented a concoction of Ensure and Häagen-Dazs ice cream, rich with calories and fat. I convinced myself that if he ate what I fed him, he would not die. He always ate a spoonful or two and pretended for my sake that he would finish the rest in a little while. But he never did. Despite my blueberry Danish and Ensure milkshakes, on a gray April morning, my father died.

That was more than twenty years ago. Even now, past the age of sixty, when I need to make a decision of consequence or heal a wound of the heart, I long for my father's advice, his stories, his easy smile. He used to take my hand in his big one, the tattoo from his days as a teenage runaway faded beneath the blond hair on his forearm, and tell me it would be all right. "Whatever it is," he always said, "we can get through it."

On days when I need that reassurance, I reach for the box of Shake 'n Bake I keep on my pantry shelf and make pork chops with it like my father did. Once a friend stopped by and watched in horror as I placed them on a plate and added a side of Rice-A-Roni. "Really?" she said in disbelief. Yes, everything was too salty, too thick on the tongue. But I love those flavors, the chemical smell of the spice pack, and even the comforting sound of the chops bouncing around in that plastic bag filled with who knows what.

When I'm feeling really low, I open my recipe box and take out the index card with the heading "Baked Macaroni à la Poops!" The nickname came from our time in Virginia, where the Bolivian family downstairs called their father Papi, which somehow morphed into Poops for my father. The paper is splotched with sauce, the ink faded to pale blue. But as I stand at the stove stirring the American cheese into the white sauce, I begin to feel better. By the time I pull the pan from the oven, the Progresso bread crumbs golden brown on top, and take my first bite, I can almost feel my father's hand. I can almost hear him laughing. The baked macaroni is filling. And wonderful. It feeds me still.

BAKED MACARONI À LA POOPS

My father loved *The Fannie Farmer Cookbook*. Fannie Farmer was a real person, born in 1857, who wrote the *Boston Cooking-*

School Cookbook in 1896. That book had almost two thousand recipes in it, and was the first to implement the use of standardized measurements such as cups and teaspoons. I guess my father was right when he'd say, "Whatever I want to make, I can find it in the *Fannie Farmer*." He used that cookbook so much that his copy fell apart. Pages were missing, and other pages had gotten smeared with something or gotten wet enough that the recipes were impossible to read. However, my guess is that his baked macaroni recipe came from that cookbook. I tried to find which edition he used, but the cover was long gone, and all I can say for certain is that it was a paperback. This recipe is the one masterpiece my father made. My kids grew up loving it, and it's a standard side dish every Thanksgiving. If the idea of using American cheese makes you queasy, substitute cheddar. Or do what my niece Melissa does and use half American, half cheddar.

Serves 6 to 8 as a main course, 8 to 10 as a side dish

INGREDIENTS

> *1 pound elbow macaroni*
> *2 sticks butter*
> *6 tablespoons flour*
> *4½ cups milk*
> *1 teaspoon dry mustard*
> *1 teaspoon celery salt*
> *Black pepper to taste*
> *1 pound American cheese, diced and divided into two portions*
> *1 cup bread crumbs*

1. Preheat the oven to 350 degrees F.
2. Cook the elbow macaroni in boiling water and drain. Set aside.

For the sauce:
3. Melt 1 stick of butter.
4. Add the flour and blend with a whisk.
5. Add the milk, dry mustard, celery salt, and black pepper and stir.
6. Bring the mixture to a boil and then add half the American cheese and stir till melted.
7. Move the macaroni to a large ceramic bowl, pour the sauce over it, and transfer the mixture to a buttered baking dish.
8. Put the remaining half pound of American cheese on top.

For the topping:
9. Melt the remaining stick of butter.
10. Place bread crumbs in a bowl and pour the melted butter over them.
11. Stir to mix, and sprinkle the bread crumbs on top of the macaroni.
12. Bake the macaroni for about half an hour.

Carbonara Quest

In the Italian American household where I grew up, red sauce ruled. Every Monday, my grandmother Mama Rose made gallons of it in a giant tarnished pot. She started that sauce by cooking sausage in oil, then frying onions in that same oil and adding various forms of canned tomatoes: crushed, pureed, paste. Without measuring, she'd toss in secret ingredients. Red wine. Sugar. Salt and pepper. Parsley from her garden. Always stirring and tasting and shaking her head, dissatisfied, until finally she got it just right. At which point the sauce simmered until, as Mama Rose used to say, it wasn't bitter.

On Mondays, my after-school snack was always that freshly made sauce on slabs of bread, a taste sensation that I have never been able to duplicate. For the rest of the week, red sauce topped chicken, veal, pasta, meatballs, and even fried eggs for those Eggs in Purgatory, which we ate on Friday nights when we Catholics had to abstain from meat. We ate our pasta and all of our parmigianas, from chicken to eggplant, drenched in sauce. There was always a gravy dish of extra sauce on the table, and we used it liberally.

Such were my southern Italian roots. And until I was out of college and working as an international flight attendant for TWA, to me Italian food was always red. I had no idea that Italy was really a country of regions, with each region proud of and exclusive to its own cooking. Of course I had general knowledge of Italian history, and I could place Florence and Rome and Venice correctly on its boot shape. But the particulars of each region and its cuisine were a mystery to me.

In those days, I was ignorant about a lot of things. I'd led a fairly protected life in my small hometown in Rhode Island, surrounded by other southern Italian immigrants. We went to what was called *the Italian church*. Little old ladies dressed in black walked the streets of my neighborhood clutching rosary beads. The music there was the sound of our harsh Neapolitan accents, the perfume the smells of the grapes and tomatoes that, just like in the old country, grew in our backyards. Wine was red and made in basements, served cold. It was so bad that I never even considered ordering wine at a restaurant until I was well into my twenties.

Suddenly, at the age of twenty-one, with a degree in English from the state university, I found myself in a Ralph Lauren uniform flying all over the world feeding passengers on 747s. I learned how to get around Paris on the Métro. I tasted razor clams in Lisbon and *moules frites* in Brussels. I got used to buying Chanel No. 5 and Dom Pérignon in duty-free shops in international airports. Still, whenever I went home for a visit, I wanted spaghetti and meatballs in red sauce for dinner. Mama Rose had died by then, and now it was my mother stirring that pot of sauce until she got the perfect combination of flavors, simmering it all day, and letting me dip bread into it when it was finally ready.

The first time I had a layover in Rome, I imagined that the food there, the spaghetti, would somehow be even more heavenly than what I had grown up eating.

Struggling with the unfamiliar items on the menu, for some reason I ordered spaghetti carbonara. I suppose I thought that spaghetti would be safe, familiar. Because for all my newly found confidence and sophistication, truth be told I was often struck by homesickness during those early days of flying. Jet lag kept me up all night in unfamiliar hotel rooms. My junior status kept me on reserve, so that I never knew when I would be working or where I'd be going, which led to me flying with different crews every time. Many layovers found me on my own, wandering the streets of a foreign city, trying to muster the courage to go into a restaurant or café or museum alone. Eventually, I grew used to this upside-down life spent mostly by myself, but for the first year or so, thrust into the big, wide world after such a sheltered life, it was often difficult.

Perhaps on that afternoon in Rome, I believed spaghetti would span the miles between me and my family, connect us in some way.

Instead, what the officious waiter in the bow tie put in front of me was yellow. And speckled with brown instead of red.

"Uh," I managed, "I ordered the spaghetti carbonara?"

What followed was a rush of dramatic Italian, much pointing to the menu and the spaghetti, and then the waiter's departure, in a huff and without my plate of spaghetti.

I was hungry.

I was alone in Rome, the rest of the crew asleep or off shopping for cheap designer handbags.

What could I do, but eat?

I took my first tentative bite, and what I tasted was maybe the most delicious thing I had ever had. Salty with cheese and bacon, creamy with eggs, the spaghetti perfectly al dente like nothing I had experienced before. I tried to thank the waiter, to explain my folly in trying to send it back, but he ignored me. I didn't really care. I had discovered something new, something delicious. I left that restaurant in love with spaghetti carbonara.

In those days, I was not much of a cook. But I knew I needed to learn to make carbonara. I scoured cookbooks and tried different versions of the dish. Back then, Italian cookbooks were few, and for some reason I could only find terrible recipes that used cream, or added mushrooms or onions. None of them were even close to the blissful dish I'd eaten in Rome.

Then, one day in a bookstore in Boston, I found an old cookbook filled with the recipes of Rome. I looked at the one for spaghetti carbonara; it was devoid of anything except bacon, eggs, and cheese. I bought the book, and the ingredients, and made it that very night.

We all know that when we have a perfect meal in a perfect faraway city, we can never quite duplicate the taste. But that night, I came close. And I used that recipe for every dinner party I had over the next couple of decades. Or, I should say, some version of it, because over time I lost that cookbook. Though it didn't really matter, because by then I'd tweaked the recipe enough—increasing the bacon, decreasing the cheese, changing the proportions each time—to make it my own, just like my mother did with her meatballs.

Spaghetti carbonara has become my comfort food, the food I make when I'm lonely like I was that long-ago afternoon in Rome, the food I make when I want to welcome others into my home. I still love my red sauce, and I dip my bread into that simmering pot on my mother's stove. But to me, spaghetti carbonara is the food not of my youth, but of my first steps into adulthood.

MY PERFECT SPAGHETTI CARBONARA

I am begging you, please do not put cream in your carbonara sauce. Don't even order carbonara in a restaurant if cream is used. The creaminess comes from the magical alchemy of Parmesan cheese and eggs and pasta water. Once I went to a dinner party where carbonara was served and it not only had cream, it also had mushrooms! Which is, I suppose, fine, if it's not called carbonara but instead is described as pasta with a mushroom-and-bacon cream sauce. However, feel free to use a pasta other than spaghetti, such as rigatoni or anything with the shape and ridges to hold the sauce. In Italy, there are somewhere between 260 and 350 types of pasta—the number varies with your source—and they are specifically designed with the purpose of clinging to a particular sauce in mind. It is said that the best carbonara is made with *guanciale*, which is cured pork jowl, or cheeks. Since this isn't typically available at your local Stop & Shop, pancetta can be substituted. But I am a big advocate of using very good bacon. Do not put butter or oil on the cooked pasta—that prevents the sauce from clinging to the pasta. And be sure to cook the pasta only until al dente, which is usually about 9 minutes. But you can only be sure by tasting. I once had a date fling some spaghetti against the kitchen wall to see if it was cooked; this method, though dramatic, proved fallible.

Serves 6

INGREDIENTS

1 pound spaghetti or other pasta

Salt

A drizzle of olive oil

1 pound bacon, chopped

3 eggs, with another 1 or 2 optional

Black pepper

1 cup Parmesan cheese, plus more for sprinkling on top

1. Cook the spaghetti in rapidly boiling water to which a big handful of salt has been added.
2. While the pasta is cooking, pour that drizzle of olive oil into a frying pan and heat it until hot.
3. Add the chopped bacon and cook over medium heat until browned.
4. Remove from the heat.
5. Beat the eggs until yellow and frothy.
6. Drain the al dente pasta, saving ¼ cup of the cooking water.
7. Put the drained pasta in your prettiest bowl.
8. Add the cooking water and eggs and toss vigorously.
9. Add the cooked bacon and toss vigorously again.
10. Add the black pepper and the cup of cheese and toss yet again.
11. If the pasta does not look creamy enough or you just feel decadent, add 1 to 2 egg yolks and toss again.
12. Sprinkle with more cheese.
13. Eat and swoon.

I love the carbonara at Otto in Greenwich Village. There they add curls of scallion on top, which looks pretty and adds a little kick to the dish.

PASTA AMATRICIANA

My daughter Annabelle prefers carbonara, but my son, Sam, prefers amatriciana. Amatriciana comes from the small town of Amatrice, which, sadly, was in the news in 2016 when an earthquake nearly destroyed it. I've been told that it is a dish to keep you warm and was fed to shepherds in the Apennine Mountains. Carbonara's roots are less traceable. Though it's known as a Roman dish, some people also trace it to the Apennine region, where woodcutters used charcoal for fuel. *Carbonara* translates to "in the style of coal," so other stories link it to something coal miners ate. And still others link it to the food shortages after the liberation of Rome; Allied forces handed out bacon and powdered eggs, which the Romans put on stored dried pasta. What I do know for sure is that both sauces use bacon (or *guanciale* or pancetta). I always have pasta and bacon on hand because either dish is easy for a weeknight meal. Traditionally, amatriciana is made with bucatini, a long spaghetti-like pasta with a hole running through the center of its length, which is how I prefer it. However, I can't always find bucatini in the grocery store, so feel free to substitute spaghetti or any short pasta that will hold the sauce.

Serves 6

INGREDIENTS

1 pound bucatini or other pasta
1 pound bacon, chopped

2 to 3 tablespoons olive oil

1 small red onion, sliced

28 ounces diced canned tomatoes, preferably San Marzano

¼ to ½ teaspoon crushed red pepper

Salt and pepper to taste

1 cup grated Parmesan, plus more for serving

1. Cook the bucatini until al dente in rapidly boiling water to which a good handful of salt has been added.
2. Cook the chopped bacon in the olive oil until crisp; remove with a slotted spoon to a plate.
3. Cook the onion in the oil and bacon drippings.
4. Remove the pan from the heat and add the tomatoes, crushed red pepper, and salt and pepper.
5. Return the pan to the stove and simmer for twenty minutes.
6. Add the bacon to the tomato mixture.
7. Drain the cooked pasta and place it in a pretty bowl.
8. Pour the tomato-bacon mixture over the pasta, stir in the Parmesan cheese, and mix very well.
9. Serve with passed bowls of extra cheese and crushed red pepper for those who like more kick.

Sausage on Wheels

Long before the Dessert Truck and Kogi Korean BBQ and the Grilled Cheese Grill, before the Mighty Cone and Frysmith, there was Sausage on Wheels.

No one would ever call my parents trendsetters. My father wore Harris tweed to work as the operations manager for the IRS in Government Center in downtown Boston, and flannel shirts and jeans on weekends. My mother still favors Liz Claiborne for dressing up. Other than the Italian food my grandmother made, we ate the staples of the 1960s: meatloaf made with Lipton dried onion soup, canned vegetables, hot dogs and hamburgers cooked on the backyard grill. My parents drove Chevys, watched *Hee Haw*; they drank whiskey sours and Michelob, line-danced and played Bingo. Yet in 1979, my safe, predictable parents bought a truck, converted the cab into a kitchen, and sold sausage-and-pepper sandwiches and meatball grinders from it.

I had forgotten about Sausage on Wheels because, I admit, their business venture had embarrassed me. I was twenty-two that year and trying on a new self, a more worldly and sophisticated one. I drank Chablis and wore Gloria Vander-bilt jeans. I dated young lawyers who drove Porsches and took me to dinner at expensive restaurants. I lived on the sixth floor of a soaring high-rise on the waterfront in Boston, just one T stop from Logan airport, where I was based as a TWA flight attendant. How could two parents who drove a truck to a flea market every Sunday to sell sandwiches ever fit into the world I was so carefully trying to create?

But one summer many years later in Portland, Oregon, I followed a map carefully marked by the hotel concierge to a parking lot where people sold food out of their trucks. I stood, surrounded by trucks selling Wiener schnitzel sand-wiches and sushi and Thai noodles and Mongolian beef and sliders and tacos. Truck food was hot. It was hip. The trend was spreading east. On that sunny day in that parking lot, I remembered Sausage on Wheels and the energetic hope and pride with which my parents ran it.

Sausage on Wheels made money. Not enough for them to quit their real jobs working for the IRS, but enough for them to take trips to Las Vegas, to give both my brother and me down payments for houses. "Even if it didn't make a dime," my father told me, "I would still do it. I love it that much." I smiled tightly while he dreamed of expanding. "Couldn't you see a Sausage on Wheels downtown?" he said, his eyes gleaming. "All those people on their lunch breaks?" I could imagine it, and the idea made me shudder. What if someone recognized them?

My parents never did expand. Instead, life got in the way. In June 1982, my brother, Skip, died suddenly. A few days later, we sat, stunned, on the back porch of our house. Sausage on Wheels was parked in the driveway. My father got up and went into the house, returning with the restaurant-sized bowl he used for mixing the meatballs. My mother joined him as he went back to the kitchen. Together, crying, they sliced peppers and onions and rolled hundreds of meatballs. The next day, they drove the truck to the flea market to sell the food they'd made.

I have a picture, a Polaroid, of my parents smiling out from the truck on its first day in business. The words SAUSAGE ON WHEELS are painted in fat letters on the side. They are happy and proud, holding sandwiches out the window. When I look at that snapshot, I wonder what they would have thought had they been able to see the future: the food trucks parked everywhere in cities across the country. Or perhaps they would be satisfied that in their ordinary way, they taught me something extraordinary. That even in grief, we must take tentative steps back into the world. That even in grief, we must eat. And that when we share that food with others, we are reclaiming those broken bits of our lives, holding them out as if to say, *I am still here. Comfort me.* As if with each bite, we remember how it is to live.

GLORIA AND HOOD'S
SAUSAGE AND PEPPERS

My mother no longer remembers how many pounds of peppers and sausages they made every weekend for Sausage on Wheels. She does remember that the sandwiches sold for two dollars each, and they brought home about a thousand dollars a weekend. So that's five hundred sandwiches. The math is mind-boggling. This recipe is for sausage and peppers, which can be served on a roll, like they used to do, for a grinder or eaten as lunch without bread. They used to add onions—sacks of them, my mother told me when I asked how many—to theirs. I like mine without. But if you do add onions, slice them not too thin and cook them, like the peppers, in the sausage drippings.

Serves 4

INGREDIENTS

   3 to 4 tablespoons olive oil
   1 pound sausage, hot or sweet or—my favorite—mixed
   2 red peppers, sliced not too thin
   2 green peppers, sliced not too thin
   Salt and pepper

1. Preheat the oven to 350 degrees F.
2. Pour the olive oil into a frying pan.

3. Roll each sausage in the oil to coat, then put them on a sheet pan and bake until browned. *Note from Gogo: Don't prick the sausage; it dries them out!*

4. Heat the olive oil over medium to medium-high heat and add the sliced peppers and salt and pepper.

5. Cook the peppers until they soften, about 10 minutes; do not remove them from the pan.

6. When the sausage is browned, add it to the peppers, either sliced into one-inch disks or whole.

7. Save the sausage drippings in an empty coffee can for future use (see "Gogo's Meatballs," page 30).

8. Serve at room temperature or hot, for lunch on its own or in a grinder, with or without onions.

Dinner for One

Back in the 1980s, I lived alone in New York City. First in a tiny apartment in a pink building on Sullivan Street, then in an almost as tiny apartment on West Twenty-first Street in Chelsea, and finally in a one-bedroom co-op on the seedy end of Bleecker Street. The neighborhood is called NoHo now, but when I moved there in 1983 it was just a nameless stretch of warehouses, with one bodega, and not much else, around the corner on Broadway. This is why I could finally afford to buy an apartment in a doorman building.

A U-Haul arrived with my furniture, which had been in storage while I sublet those other apartments. When the movers brought it in, I was surprised by how much I hated all my old things. Living in New York City had changed me in many ways—I'd learned who Sam Shepard was, I walked miles every day, I'd boldly moved into this godforsaken neighborhood, and I'd developed my own taste in clothes and music and, I realized as my blue-flowered couch appeared, in furniture. Everything I owned had been bought to imitate what my friends back in Boston had. By the time the moving truck pulled up to 77 Bleecker Street, I'd abandoned my Ralph Lauren polo shirts and khaki pants for black. Now I had to abandon this ugly furniture.

That first day in my new apartment, I went to the Grand Union supermarket a few blocks away and bought bags of food: roasts and chops, bacon and eggs, pasta and rice and potatoes and cheese and fresh vegetables and New York apples and a crate of clementines (a fruit I'd never seen until it began to appear at the corner bodega my first fall in Manhattan). I figured that I might have the most embarrassing furniture in all of Manhattan, but at least my refrigerator and cupboards were full.

When my parents called that night, I explained that I couldn't talk because I was making dinner.

"What are you making?" my mother asked.

"A pork roast, mashed potatoes, asparagus."

Always worried about her twenty-six-year-old daughter alone in an unsafe neighborhood in an unsafe city (this was 1983, after all), she said, "Oh good! You're having company!"

"No, it's just me." My oven dinged, letting me know it was ready for the roast. "Got to go," I said, and quickly hung up.

That night, I set the square oak table I'd inherited from an old boyfriend in Boston, poured a glass of chardonnay, and lit candles, beginning my habit of cooking good, full meals for myself almost every night. By the time I got married and had kids, I had shelves of cookbooks and a recipe box with the recipes I'd torn from newspapers and magazines. Chicken paella. Curried chicken with pear chutney. Teriyaki flank steak. Chilaquiles. Beef stew. Turkey in mole. Artichoke soup. The pork roast I made that first night on Bleecker Street. All of it honed in my little galley kitchen.

I understand now that those elaborate meals cooked and eaten alone were my way of staving off loneliness and keeping sadness at bay. Earlier that summer, when I'd moved into that tiny apartment on Sullivan Street, my brother Skip—five years older and my only sibling—had died suddenly in an accident. My grief-stricken parents had urged me to fulfill my dream of moving to Manhattan and pursuing a life as a writer. "You can't stay here and take care of us for the rest of your life," they told me. I loved my new life—the off-off-Broadway plays, the Indian restaurants on East Sixth Street, the readings at Three Lives bookstore, the long aimless walks and all the hours spent browsing at the Strand Book Store. But sometimes my sadness was so big I felt everyone I passed could see it. Once, as I was walking home with a new stack of books, a stranger stopped to ask me if I was okay. When I told him I was fine, he said, "I'm sorry. You just look so sad."

In my new life a decade later—husband, children, drafty Victorian in Providence, Rhode Island, with a giant 1919 Glenwood stove—I cooked out of joy. I actually thought in those early days of babies and passionate love that I was the happiest person ever. My cooking repertoire got kid-friendly recipes added to it. I made homemade applesauce on that big old stove, and homemade mac and cheese, and "cheesy potatoes," which were potatoes au gratin from Patricia Wells's *Bistro Cooking*. I cooked to nurture my growing family, to hear my husband moan with pleasure at the taste of my ginger salmon, to see my kids reach for seconds and even thirds. I cooked and cooked and cooked, happily.

Of course, such joy doesn't always last. It can't, can it? From where I am now, years later, I see all the missteps I made: being too trusting, wanting to believe in a fairy-tale marriage that I slowly learned was anything but that. Still, those discoveries and heartbreaks came later, years after we moved to a house built in 1792 with an oddly shaped kitchen. The Glenwood stove went unused; after hauling it across town, we discovered that our new house didn't have a gas hookup. I found myself having to cook on an electric stove for the first time, and dreaming of a kitchen renovation that never happened. Looking back, I can see that even then my husband and I were drifting apart. Many nights I was cooking for just the kids and me, my husband making excuses for not coming home, Grace standing on a stool to help stir sauces and Sam carefully following a recipe beside me.

When Grace died suddenly in 2002, from a virulent form of strep, for the first time in two decades I stopped cooking altogether and let friends and neighbors feed my family and me. It was months before I returned to my kitchen, trying to remember how to make something as simple as spaghetti. Once, I had cooked out of loneliness. Once, out of joy. Now I was cooking to keep from losing my mind from grief. I began making more and more complicated recipes, driving to ethnic markets for ingredients. Dinner took hours, sometimes even days, to make. I marinated and rolled and simmered and kneaded. I cooked to save my life.

One day I looked up and life had changed yet again. Our son Sam was all grown up, out of college and living in Brooklyn, often calling me for some recipe he wanted to try. Our daughter Annabelle was in middle school. And, despite my desperate attempts to hold on, to stay a family, to fix it, our marriage was in tatters. There wasn't a recipe in any of those stained and dog-eared cookbooks that could rescue it. At almost sixty, I found myself once again standing in an empty apartment, waiting for a moving truck.

This time, when my pale blue sofa and crazy patterned chairs arrived, I smiled. My art, carefully chosen from trips to Cuba and Colombia and Argentina or bought from artist friends, reminded me how far I'd traveled since that apartment on Bleecker Street. It took days to unpack all my boxes, a lifetime of belongings waiting to go into cupboards and closets, onto new shelves and tabletops. Annabelle went on a road trip with her dad that week while I set up our new home.

Alone for the first time there, looking out at a new landscape of industrial buildings and smokestacks instead of historically restored houses, I reached for my orange Le Creuset baking pan and did the thing that always comforted me: I cooked. I cut slits into a pork roast and stuffed those slits with sliced garlic. I showered the meat with salt and pepper and put it in the oven. I boiled Yukon Gold potatoes until they were tender, then whipped them with milk and butter and salt and pepper. I roasted slender stalks of asparagus, tossed in good olive oil and salt, beside that roast. My new home grew rich with the smells of good food that I cooked to nourish myself. I lit candles and set the table for one with the Fiesta ware I'd collected over a lifetime and one of the napkins I'd bought in Lyon. I poured a glass of cabernet and filled my plate.

I paused to think about what I had lost, what I had left behind. But what do you say about a marriage that ends? How do you point to those places when it started to crack? That night, I tried to do that. I tried to understand the man I had thought I knew. The man I had loved so hard once. But in my case, I still had more questions than answers. His actions remained a mystery to me, as did why I'd put up with his emotional withdrawal for so long.

My mother called to be sure I was okay. "I'm great," I said. "I'm just sitting down to eat." She laughed. "Did you make yourself a big dinner?" she asked, as she had that day I'd moved into my apartment alone in the city. I told her that in fact I had. After we hung up, I looked around—at my new home, at my dinner, at the city lights now twinkling outside my window. I was cooking for one again. But all these years later, I was cooking not out of sadness or joy or grief. I was cooking out of hope. I was cooking to feed myself, and I was so hungry.

PORK ROAST WITH GARLIC

This recipe is so easy that you can see why I made it a lot when I lived alone, as well as after I had kids and was feeding a family. It is best served with mashed potatoes and gravy made from the drippings. Just remove the pork from the pan, and while it's resting heat the drippings on the stove, right in the same pan. Add about ¼ cup of flour to the drippings and stir it up to make a roux, then slowly pour in milk until it's smooth and looks like gravy. Add salt and pepper to taste.

Serves 4 to 6

INGREDIENTS

A 2- to 3-pound boneless center-cut pork loin
Lots of garlic, peeled—enough to fill all the slits you make
Salt and pepper

1. Preheat the oven to 375 degrees F.
2. With a sharp knife, cut small slits all over the pork roast.
3. Shove a garlic clove deep into each slit.
4. Salt and pepper the pork generously.
5. Roast in roasting pan for 40 minutes, or until a thermometer inserted in the center registers 145 degrees F.
6. Let rest for 15 to 20 minutes, during which you can make your gravy and mashed potatoes (by dumping 4 to 6 quartered cooked potatoes, skin on, into your food pro-

cessor and whipping them up with a stick of butter, some milk or cream, and salt and pepper).

Enchiladas

When you make a pork roast for one person, there will be leftovers. Plenty of leftovers. The next day for lunch, I like to take some thick slices of pork and make either an open-faced sandwich—toasted white bread, pork, leftover gravy, all warmed up—or a regular pork sandwich with mustard. And still I will have more leftovers, which, a couple of days later (so that I have a pork break), I'll incorporate into enchiladas, which are the best way I know to use up leftover pork, chicken, or beef. I like to use green enchilada sauce for pork and chicken, and red for beef.

NOHO PORK ENCHILADAS

INGREDIENTS

Leftover pork, at least 3 or 4 thick slices

Corn tortillas

1 tablespoon canola oil

1 tablespoon flour

Green enchilada sauce, preferably Hatch

1 cup of chicken broth

2 cups shredded cheese: cheddar, Monterey jack, or a combi-
     nation; but please don't use cheese with spices mixed into it

Diced white onion

Sour cream

Chopped cilantro (optional)

1. Preheat the oven to 350 degrees F.
2. Dice the leftover pork into bite-sized pieces.
3. Wrap 3 or 4 tortillas at a time in a dampened paper towel and warm for 30 seconds in the microwave to make them soft and pliable. Keep them covered.
4. Heat the canola oil and add the flour, stirring to make a roux.
5. Add the green enchilada sauce and the chicken broth, stir, and let simmer for one minute. Turn off the heat.
6. In the bottom of a roasting dish, spread a thin layer of the sauce.
7. Fill the tortillas, one at a time, with about ¼ cup of pork and a big pinch of shredded cheese.
8. Roll the tortillas up tight and place them in the pan seam side down.
9. When the pan is full, with the enchiladas nestled close together, pour the remaining sauce over the top and then sprinkle with about 1 cup of cheese.
10. Bake until bubbling, about twenty minutes.
11. Add the diced onion and cilantro, if desired.
12. Serve with dollops of sour cream.

NOHO CHICKEN ENCHILADAS

I used to make chicken enchiladas from a recipe I saw in *Glamour* magazine. I've lost the recipe, but I still remember the secret ingredient—cream cheese!—that made them so good. Here's my version of that recipe.

INGREDIENTS

4 to 5 chopped scallions, with some reserved for serving
1 small can chopped, roasted chiles
16 ounces cream cheese, softened
Corn tortillas
1 tablespoon canola oil
1 tablespoon flour
Green enchilada sauce, preferably Hatch
1 cup of chicken broth
Leftover chicken (at least 2 breasts), diced into bite-sized
  pieces
2 cups shredded cheese: cheddar, Monterey jack, or a combi-
  nation; but please don't use cheese with spices mixed into it
Sour cream

1. Preheat the oven to 350 degrees F.
2. In a bowl, mix most of the scallions (remembering to save some for serving) and the chiles into the softened cream cheese.
3. Wrap 3 or 4 tortillas at a time in a dampened paper towel

and warm for 30 seconds in the microwave to make them soft and pliable. Keep them covered.

4. Heat the canola oil and add the flour, stirring to make a roux.

5. Add the green enchilada sauce and the chicken broth, stir, and let simmer for one minute. Turn off the heat.

6. In the bottom of a roasting dish, spread a thin layer of the sauce.

7. Fill the tortillas, one at a time, with a scant ¼ cup of chicken, a tablespoon of the cream cheese mixture, and a big pinch of shredded cheese.

8. Roll the tortillas up tight and place them in the pan seam side down.

9. When the pan is full, with the enchiladas nestled close together, pour the remaining sauce over the top and then sprinkle with about 1 cup of cheese.

10. Bake until bubbling, about twenty minutes.

11. Serve with dollops of sour cream and the remaining scallions.

Party Like It's 1959

When I was a child, dinner parties seemed to belong to some vague and distant grown-up world where women wore shiny dresses with tight bodices and full skirts, bright lipstick, and strings of perfect pearls. The men, I imagined, wore ties and wingtips. They drank fancy cocktails and ate prime rib on heavy china. This image came from Saturday afternoon movies and glossy magazines, pictures of an adult world I could only peek into.

Now that I'm a grown-up, my dinner parties look nothing like the ones I used to imagine. My plates are colorful Fiesta ware. The drink of choice is wine—red or white. No one is very dressed up. And the food is always an experiment. I give my guests chimichurri sauce, ginger martinis, Israeli couscous, green-chile tamales, paella. When I go to dinner parties, I'm served tandoori chicken, Moroccan tagines, and spaghetti—carbonara, puttanesca, or arrabbiata. I'm served family-style, with make-your-own pizzas or tacos.

That is, this format held until a Saturday night in the early 1990s.

That night, my then husband and I drove to a house in a cul-de-sac. Our host and hostess were an older couple, he in a snappy tie, she in pearls. Their house was in a suburb known for its good schools and manicured yards. But they were jolly and refined, old hands at entertaining. We stepped into a sunken living room. We were offered a drink. "White wine," I said. "Tom Collins," one of the other women said. "Whiskey sour," said another. "Martini. Up. Extra olives," said a third. The host dipped into an alcove where a complete bar awaited him, and he proceeded to shake, stir, chill, garnish, and—yawn—pour (that would be my white wine). The Tom Collins sat pretty and pink in a tall glass with a maraschino cherry floating happily inside. The whiskey sour had froth. Three olives bobbed in the martini.

We sat down to nibble Ritz crackers and a log of cheddar cheese rolled in chopped walnuts. A silver tray of shrimp and cocktail sauce was passed around. When I was growing up, my parents didn't have dinner parties, but if they had, this is what they would have been like. I started to grow nostalgic for something I'd never experienced.

We were called into the dining room for dinner. A white tablecloth. Silver candlesticks with white candles already lit. The table set with real china: ivory with a border of pink flowers and a silver band around the edges. On top of each dinner plate sat a fluted clear salad plate, the first course already served and waiting. I thought, fleetingly, of my too-heavy wooden salad bowl filled with baby lettuce and shaved Parmesan and maybe fennel. This salad was iceberg lettuce, one wedge of tomato, and one perfect circle of cucumber, all of it coated with Good Seasons salad dressing, the one you mix in its own cruet.

I would recognize it anywhere, that dressing. Its speckles of red and black, its greasy sheen. In college, my roommates and I played grown-up by cooking dinner for our boyfriends. We marinated London broil in that same salad dressing and served it with Rice-A-Roni, the San Francisco treat. For dessert, we gave them ice cream with canned cherries dumped on top and doused with brandy, which we then lit. Cherries Jubilee! Our dessert was flambé! And so were we, college kids all on fire, eating this fancy dinner just as a prelude to sex. On those Saturday nights, we traded in our blue jeans for dresses, and wore lip gloss and blush. We were not yet sure what real adults did at dinner parties, but we felt our way along, playing Frank Sinatra records and struggling for mature conversation around the table. I hadn't thought of those college dinner parties in years, but this dinner party in the cul-de-sac was doing funny things to me. It was making me wistful. It was making me remember how I used to love kissing a boy named David all night after that Cherries Jubilee.

Main course. The host appeared with a large platter that

matched the rest of the china—I saw the silver edge peeking out from beneath a chateaubriand ringed with asparagus cooked so thoroughly they appeared to be asleep, small new potatoes, and ridged disks of bright orange carrots. It was so beautiful, I had the urge to cry, though I'm not certain why. "How do you like your meat?" the host asked, hovering beside me with that gorgeous platter of food. I wanted to take it from him and eat it all. But of course I didn't. I said, "Rare," and he placed two perfectly cooked rare slices on my dinner plate, along with the vegetables and—what was this the hostess was handing me in a sterling silver gravy boat? I took it from her, looked inside, and found béarnaise sauce, thick and yellow and flecked with tarragon.

My wineglass was filled with red wine. My dinner was before me. I gazed at it and was struck by a sense of familiarity so strong I couldn't put my knife and fork to the meat. I was paralyzed by memory. I had had this dinner, this very dinner—chateaubriand with béarnaise sauce and asparagus and new potatoes and carrots—many times before. But when? Where?

Then I remembered. This was the exact dinner we used to serve on transcontinental flights in first class on TWA in 1978 when I was a flight attendant. I placed the white linen napkins on the tray tables, making sure the red TWA logo was in the lower right-hand corner, facing the passenger. I wheeled my dinner cart into the aisle and carved the chateaubriand in front of the entire first class. It was air travel as theater. And for me, a twenty-one-year-old from a small town in Rhode Island, it was the height of sophistication. Aha! I thought, standing at the front of that first-class cabin gazing at the passengers. This is what the adult world looks like, what they eat, how they travel. It was as shiny and beautiful as I had imagined as a little girl.

Even in coach on long-haul flights, the meal service ended with an after-dinner drink cart. Liqueurs arranged on top of those white linen napkins, red TWA logo facing out, miniature bottles of amaretto, Grand Marnier, Kahlúa, B&B, all standing there beside small after-dinner drink glasses. In flight attendant training, we had had to pass a test in which we correctly identified all of those liqueurs without their labels, which, we were told, fell off when they got wet. With my eyes closed I could recognize the slender triangle of Galliano, the squat amaretto, the Frangelico monk.

We put a piece of dry ice on that cart, sprinkled it with water, and had our own homemade fog machine. I strolled down the aisles of a Lockheed L-1011 in a mist of glamour and promise, the children's eyes widening with wonder, businessmen opening their wallets, wives asking husbands, Which should I get? We asked unaccompanied minors or well-behaved kids to follow us with a tray of gold foil–wrapped TWA mints; inside, the green was as pale as the crème de menthe we were offering.

Finally, I returned to this dinner party, dizzy for what I once had, what I never had, what I had hoped for. Dizzy with nostalgia for those long-ago kisses that tasted like canned cherries, for the glamour of flying to Los Angeles in a fog of dry ice, for the twenty-one-year-old girl I once was, standing in front of thirty first-class passengers in my Ralph Lauren uniform and black pumps carving a chateaubriand into perfect slices to a round of applause.

As an adult, I know that how we entertain is a combination of who we are and how we live, of all the dinners we've had and all the dreams we still embrace. But on that night in the house with the sunken living room, at the place I once yearned to be, I am happy to cut my meat with the heavy wedding silver. I put it into my mouth, and—finally—I savor it.

Michael's Whiskey Sours

My husband, Michael, not unlike those men and women at the dinner parties of the 1950s and '60s, likes a cocktail hour before dining. At home, this means he whips up negronis or Manhattans for us, and we sit sipping our drinks and nibbling cheese. But my favorite of all the cocktails he makes for me is the whiskey sour. The negronis and Manhattans I typically get in restaurants are quite good. The whiskey sours, not so much. But Michael's whiskey sour, like Michael himself, is pretty damned perfect. More about that later, in "Three Potato," where you will also learn that he makes the only baked potato I've ever liked.

MICHAEL'S WHISKEY SOURS

This recipe uses simple syrup, which is simply ½ cup of sugar and ½ cup of water microwaved until the sugar is dissolved. It can be adjusted for any number of servings by using the ratio of 4 parts bourbon to 1 part citrus juice and 1 part simple syrup.

Serves 8

INGREDIENTS

> *3 egg whites*
> *16 ounces bourbon*
> *4 ounces simple syrup*
> *3 ounces lemon juice*
> *1 ounce lime juice*

1. Put the egg whites in a large Pyrex measuring cup and blend them using a hand blender or whisk until they are lightly foamy.
2. Add the remaining ingredients and blend or whisk again.
3. Taste and add more lemon juice or more simple syrup as needed.
4. Strain into another container, then return the strained whiskey back into the measuring cup (for easy pouring).
5. Fill the balance of the cup with ice and stir until thoroughly chilled.
6. Pour into chilled coupes or over ice in old-fashioned glasses.

Cherries Jubilee

I have to admit that I really liked the dinner-party Cherries Jubilee of my college years, though I'm certain I wouldn't be so keen on it now. The real recipe is not at all hard to make, so if you get the desire to party like it's 1959, make a batch of Michael's Whiskey Sours to start and finish up with classic Cherries Jubilee, which was invented by none other than the renowned French chef Auguste Escoffier in 1887, to honor Queen Victoria and celebrate the fiftieth year of her reign. Escoffier had already created Peach Melba for opera singer Nellie Melba and eggs scrambled in champagne for Sarah Bernhardt. Why not invent a dessert for the queen? His original dish did not include ice cream, which is how we always serve it now. Rather, it highlighted Queen Victoria's favorite fruit—the cherry—by adapting an old French technique that used sugar and brandy to preserve fruit. It's no surprise that the dessert became popular at dinner parties in the 1950s and '60s, when tipsy hostesses wowed their guests by flambèing the cherries in brandy for a dramatic ending to the meal. We are only lucky that houses and hostesses didn't flambé as well.

DINNER-PARTY CHERRIES JUBILEE

You'll want to have long matches on hand for this dish.

Makes enough for a dinner party of 6

INGREDIENTS

3 tablespoons butter

6 tablespoons sugar

6 cups dark Bing cherries, pitted and stemmed (frozen are
acceptable but please forgo the canned ones)

Juice of 1 lemon

6 tablespoons kirsch

Vanilla-bean ice cream

1. Melt the butter in a medium saucepan.
2. Add the sugar and stir until it dissolves.
3. Add the cherries.
4. Add the lemon juice.
5. Simmer until the cherry juice thickens.
6. Remove from heat and add the kirsch.
7. Immediately hold a lit match just above the surface of the cherries. The sauce must be warm to ignite.
8. Once the flame subsides, put the cherries with their juices in parfait glasses and top each with a scoop of ice cream.

Soft Food

One day the pediatrician looked at me and announced, "Sam is ready for soft food!" Of course, Sam had eaten applesauce and Gerber baby food. This was the next step in his diet—soft food that wasn't pureed or jarred. I felt the same wave of bafflement that had washed over me again and again during the six months since he'd been born. From the day I'd given birth to my son, I'd realized that I had entered a strange and foreign world. I was thirty-six years old and had traveled to four continents and dozens of countries. But never had I felt so out of my element as I did in the land of motherhood.

Until I had Sam, I had held a baby exactly once. I was navigating this new land mostly alone. Sam's father had left me during the pregnancy, vacillating almost daily between coming back and staying gone—mostly staying gone—until Sam was almost two years old and we got married. So several times a week—sometimes several times a day—I found myself on the phone to my friend Beth, who had three children and was pregnant with a fourth. "Something's happening to me!" I told her a few days after Sam and I came home from the hospital. "My breasts are hardening!" "No, no, darling," she cooed in her calming voice. "That's just your milk coming in." I called Dr. Utter, the pediatrician, a lot, too. One morning when Sam was a few weeks old, I peeked into his diaper and shrieked. As soon as Dr. Utter picked up the phone, I blurted, "I have to bring Sam in. His poop isn't mustard-colored like they describe in *What to Expect the First Year*, it's closer to chartreuse." "Well, well," Dr. Utter said, "put down the color wheel and just change the thing." My parents were nearby, and helpful in coming over to watch Sam so I could take a shower or a nap, but they, too, were fuzzy on things like what color his poop should be.

Now I was confronted with this: *soft food*.

On the way home to our second-floor apartment in a lovingly restored Colonial house, with Sam strapped into his car seat babbling happily at Pat, the androgynous black-and-white face that I'd hung in front of him for proper stimulation, I said, "Soft food, soft food, soft food. What the hell is soft food, Sam?" Since he was my constant companion, I talked to him a lot. Years later, my landlady told me she used to listen to my one-way conversations with my baby, certain he would grow up to have a great vocabulary. (He did.)

My apartment had beautiful historical details. What it didn't have was a parking place. How far that two-block walk from the lot where I rented a space felt carrying a packed diaper bag and a car seat with a baby strapped into it. I think I felt loneliest on those walks, wondering how I'd landed here, the man I'd fallen in love with AWOL and me alone in Providence, Rhode Island, nearly two hundred miles from my beloved Manhattan, where I'd lived and built a life I loved, now a single mother with no friends. Across Hope Street, past lovely homes painted Colonial colors, with historic plaques beside their front doors; across Brook Street, where, if I wasn't exhausted from raising a baby alone and trying to finish a novel, I would stop at Acme Video for a couple movies; then up the hill that was my street, Transit Street, whose name offered the possibility that this was just a transition, that soon Sam and I might land back in Manhattan; then down the long driveway of No. 101, past the garden that had boasted pale pink peonies in April, when Sam was born, and now showed off hot-pink and crimson zinnias; then up a winding flight of steep stairs, clutching the car seat and the diaper bag and still talking out loud to Sam, except now I was most likely saying, "Almost there, buddy, almost there"; and then finally flinging open the door and dropping the diaper bag and catching my breath. Home.

I am a nester, and I have always prided myself in how through fourteen moves in fifteen years I had always created a home. As soon as I walked in the door, everything felt better. Except one thing still nagged at me: *soft food*. I briefly considered skipping this step and keeping him on the baby-food squash he loved so much. But no, I was going to do this right. I took Sam out of his car seat and let him crawl around the kitchen while I stared into the refrigerator and surveyed the various food in bowls on the counter. I had hummus, which was soft. I had avocados, which when mashed and seasoned could become guacamole, which was also soft. I smiled and started to peel a Hass. "Okay, buddy," I said, "I'm going to make you lunch."

Oh, I was proud of myself! Once again I had navigated my way through the streets of motherhood. Not so long ago, I had felt smug when I'd untangled the Métro in Paris or the Underground in London. I used to study maps, my finger tracing the way to the Grand Place in Brussels or the train route that would take me to Heidelberg, Germany. But there was no map for motherhood, and each triumph made me giddy. Sam feasted on hummus and guacamole, baba ghanoush and smoked trout spread. His breath stank, and his diapers stank even worse. But he gobbled up every spoonful I offered him.

When Beth arrived one afternoon, I decided to show her how far I'd come.

"So," I said as I filled Sam's plastic dish shaped like an airplane with smoked trout in one compartment and roasted garlic hummus—his new favorite—in another, "Sam is eating soft food now."

Beth looked puzzled. "What are you feeding this baby?" she asked me.

I told her. She started to laugh. "Ann," she said, "soft food means pastina or creamy rice. Applesauce."

Applesauce? It had never occurred to me. But there was no turning back. At six months old, Sam had a palate more sophisticated than that of some adults I knew. By the time he was three, he was gobbling the prized fish eyes at a dinner party and asking for thirds of rabbit pâté in Normandy; when we visited Vietnam when he was twelve, he was the only one of us who dared to eat durian, the Asian fruit that smells like stinky feet. And by the time he was in high school, he was cooking beside me in the kitchen, chopping and sautéing and tossing.

My house salad dressing is the one Sam invented—olive oil, lemon, salt, and honey—and when I roast meats I still make Sam's Potatoes: cut-up Yukon Golds with more garlic, rosemary, and salt than seems prudent. When he comes home for a visit now from his own apartment in Brooklyn, he is always ready to cook with me. We look through cookbooks together for what I'll make: beef in Barolo or braised ribs. Something to go with his specialty—which, I wasn't surprised to learn, is polenta, that softest of soft food. We have traveled far together, Sam and I. We did move out of that apartment eventually. His father came back for a while, we added another baby, we moved into other homes. For over a decade we lived in our own Colonial house, one street parallel to that first apartment on Transit Street.

Two years ago I found myself in a new home, just my daughter Annabelle and me. But I made a room for Sam, with purple walls and books of plays and a table with a jigsaw puzzle always in the works. He stands beside me in this new kitchen, all six feet, five inches of him, stirring polenta with a long wooden spoon. "It smells like home here," he tells me when I add onion to sizzling oil, then carefully brown the meat I'm going to braise. I press my arm against his, and suddenly he is a baby in a car seat, and I am carrying him across Hope Street, I am telling him, *We are almost there, buddy*, I am pretending I am an airplane delivering garlicky hummus to his open gummy smile, I am finding my way, I am finding our way. We are home.

My Favorite Soft Foods

Two and a half decades have passed since I was a single mother trying to figure out what to feed her baby after the doctor said he was ready for soft food. Today, a better cook and a calmer mother, I would have no problem determining what soft food to make. Below are my favorite soft-food recipes, for babies and grown-ups alike.

FRENCH SCRAMBLED EGGS

My father made the most delicious scrambled eggs by adding cream and sugar to them when he was whipping the eggs together, before pouring them into the pan. But I think the scrambled eggs I make in a double boiler—often referred to as French Scrambled Eggs—are even more delicate and better-tasting. Made with cream and butter, these small, soft curds are my favorite soft food these days. Escoffier came up with the idea of cooking the eggs in a double boiler, which prevents them from browning and, therefore, results in a creamier egg. My husband can get the same results in a regular old frying pan. But for the rest of us, this method won't disappoint or challenge.

Makes 2 servings

INGREDIENTS

1 tablespoon butter

3 eggs

Salt and pepper

3 tablespoons heavy cream (if you don't have heavy cream on hand, half-and-half or whole milk works fine)

Chopped chives (optional)

1. Set up your double boiler by putting enough water in the bottom pan to just caress the top pan.
2. Get the water simmering and put the top pan on it.
3. Add the butter and let it melt.
4. Lightly beat the eggs in a small bowl with salt and pepper (white pepper is nice in these because it keeps the eggs daffodil yellow, without adding black specks)
5. Add the eggs to the melted butter.
6. You need to whisk the eggs as they cook, but the longer you wait, the larger the curds will be. If you whisk right away, you get smaller curds. This is entirely up to you.

7. When the eggs begin to set, whisk in the milk and the chives, if you have them.

8. That's it! French Scrambled Eggs! Delicious served with thick-cut bacon on the side and good toast.

NEVER-FAIL SOUFFLÉ

From *Saveur* magazine

The first thing you need to know about this soufflé is that it's not a soufflé. Maybe it's a strata. I'm not really sure, though once I was invited to a brunch where everyone had to bring a dish, so of course I brought this, because it's pretty, yummy, and people always praise it highly and ask me for the recipe. But the hostess made a strata, a complicated soufflé dish with sausages and peppers and lots of eggs. When my soufflé sat beside that strata, the hostess actually took her dish off the table. However, when you give people this recipe, they make a disgusted face. How could something this good have such mundane ingredients in it? All I can say is make it exactly like Matt Taylor-Gross instructed in *Saveur* a decade ago, and you, too, will wow a crowd. I make it every year for my mother's Easter breakfast and anytime friends stay over on a Saturday night, so that on Sunday morning we have an elegant meal of soft, cheesy eggs. It's very important that you set this up the night before you are going to bake it, and that you serve it hot. On Easter, I let it sit overnight in the fridge and then bake it at Gogo's house; that way, it's puffy and hot when it's served.

Serves 8

INGREDIENTS

A dozen eggs

2 cups half-and-half

Pinch of red pepper flakes (I leave this out because I'm often serving it to kids who can taste something spicy a mile away)

3 cups grated cheddar cheese

1 loaf white bread, crusts removed, bread cut into 1-inch cubes (I have tried this with all kinds of bread, and the cheap stuff—like Wonder bread—works best)

Salt and white pepper

6 tablespoons butter, melted

1. The night before you are going to serve this, beat the eggs, half-and-half, and crushed red pepper flakes, if you're using them, in a bowl. Set aside.
2. Sprinkle 1 cup of the cheese on the bottom of a 9-by-12-inch baking dish.
3. Cover the cheese with about two-thirds of the bread and season with salt and pepper.
4. Sprinkle another cup of cheese on top.
5. Cover this layer with the rest of the bread and salt and pepper.

6. Finish with the final cup of cheese.

7. Pour the egg mixture over the cheese and bread.

8. Drizzle the melted butter on top.

9. Refrigerate overnight.

10. About an hour before serving, take the dish out of the fridge and let it come to room temperature.

11. Preheat the oven to 350 degrees F.

12. Bake until puffed and golden, about 45 minutes.

Guacamole

If you have a baby ready for soft food, I highly recommend introducing him or her to guacamole, which is also one of my own favorite things to eat. Hold the tortilla chips until the kid is older. My husband has a simple recipe that even my fourteen-year-old daughter, Annabelle, makes on her own: Chop a shallot and let it sit in lots of lime juice for ten or fifteen minutes, mash up three or four avocados and add the shallots with most of the lime juice and some salt. Easy and soft! If you want a more complex guacamole, below is the recipe my friend Bruce Tillinghast makes, which appeared in *Christopher Kimball's Milk Street*. After I saw a friend of mine, the fabulous writer Laura Lippman, make and serve guacamole in a heavy stone mortar and pestle, I went out and got one myself. I suggest you invest in same, but until then mash with whatever you have on hand.

CENTRAL MEXICAN GUACAMOLE

Courtesy of *Christopher Kimball's Milk Street*

Too many guacamole recipes are a muddle of flavors. Diana Kennedy's use of just a handful of traditional ingredients allowed the dish's simple flavors to be the focus. White onion mashed with cilantro and serrano chiles adds the right amount of bite, while chopped grape tomatoes offer balanced acidity against the rich avocados. Mashing the cilantro, chiles, and onion in the same bowl as the avocados keeps their flavors in the food, not on the cutting board. We were surprised that we never missed the lime juice. Guacamole hinges on the ripeness of the avocados; they should be soft but slightly firm.

Don't discard the seeds from the chiles. This recipe relies on them for a pleasant heat. —J. M. Hirsch and Diane Unger

Serves 4

INGREDIENTS

4 tablespoons finely chopped fresh cilantro
1 to 2 serrano chiles, stemmed and finely chopped
2 tablespoons finely chopped white onion
Kosher salt
3 ripe avocados, halved and pitted
1 pint (10 ounces) grape tomatoes, finely chopped
Tortilla chips, to serve

In a bowl, combine 2 tablespoons of the cilantro, the chiles, the onion, and ½ teaspoon salt. Mash with the bottom of a dry measuring cup until a rough paste forms, about 1 minute. Scoop the avocado flesh into the bowl and coarsely mash with a potato masher or fork. Stir in half of the tomatoes until combined. Taste and season with salt. Transfer to a serving bowl and sprinkle with the remaining cilantro and tomatoes.

One Potato, Two

The potatoes of my childhood came two ways: mashed and baked. The mashed were buttery and smooth and always served with roast beef or pork roast, drenched in gravy. These were my brother Skip's favorite food, and after everyone else took some, he was allowed to eat them straight from the big red bowl in which they were served. All of them. This is partly why he had to buy his clothes in the husky department.

The baked potatoes were wrapped in foil, baked to death, and left to wither in the oven. Usually we had them when we had steak for dinner. We unwrapped the foil, made a slit in the potato, and dropped in a pat of margarine and then a dollop of sour cream. For this reason, I am not a fan of baked potatoes.

Until I had children, in my late thirties, I pretty much

avoided potatoes (except for French fries, which are an entirely different thing). Sometimes because of the calories, sometimes because of the overbaked ones of my youth, sometimes because wild rice just tasted better. But then along came kids and the need to cook balanced meals. Protein. Starch. Vegetable. Every single day.

It was easy to return to mashed potatoes: throw some cooked potatoes in the KitchenAid (or hand mixer) with a lot of butter and a splash of milk and a good dose of salt. But even children shouldn't eat mashed potatoes every night.

Despite this challenge, let me say here that cooking dinner for my family was my favorite part of the day. Sam and Grace would stand on their little stools and line the pie plate with sliced apples for Apple Crisp or stir the tomato sauce on the stove while I chopped and diced and boiled and sautéed. We made a happy little kitchen, the three of us, the air filled with the warm smells of roasting chicken or fresh rosemary or sweet corn cooling. We set a pretty table every night, too, each of us with our favorite color Fiesta ware plate and cotton napkins we'd bought at a market in Provence. In fact, when I asked Sam—now twenty-five—what his favorite dish of mine was, he couldn't answer. Instead, as I began to sauté onions and garlic for chili, he said, "That's what I love! Coming into the kitchen and smelling that and seeing you standing at the stove."

But back to potatoes.

Some twenty years ago, I put a chicken in the oven to roast (also so easy: shove a lemon or an apple with a head of garlic cut in half longways inside it, rub softened butter all over the skin, stick branches of fresh rosemary or tarragon or thyme or all three in the cavity and the leg joints, douse with salt and pepper, and bake at 375 degrees F until the little red thermometer pops up) and stared at the Yukon Gold potatoes on the counter.

As if reading my mind, Sam said, "Let me make them!"

Really, even though he was only four or five, I was more than willing to hand over this part of the dinner to him.

"How will you cook them?" I asked.

"In the oven!" (Sam has been an actor his whole life, so the exclamation marks are exactly how he spoke, even then.)

"I don't know, Sam, Mommy's not a fan of baked potatoes," I told him.

"Cut them up and I'll do the rest!"

So I did. I peeled the potatoes and cut them into chunks, then handed them over to Sam, who poured more olive oil and salt on them than was reasonable. He stirred them to be sure they were good and coated, tossed in some fresh rosemary sprigs, and announced that they were ready to go into the oven. Every fifteen or twenty minutes he'd peer in and decide they weren't quite done, until finally they were: crunchy and brown on the outside and soft and white inside, perfectly seasoned. Sam's Potatoes became a staple at dinner. Sometimes he added whole cloves of garlic. If we didn't have fresh rosemary, he did without any herbs. And they always came out just right.

Grace's Cheesy Potatoes, on the other hand, required more precision. To most people, "cheesy potatoes" means potatoes au gratin. But in my children's childhood home, they were Grace's Cheesy Potatoes, sliced thin, layered, and topped with shredded Gruyère and cream. The recipe came from a Patricia Wells cookbook that I received as a birthday gift. Grace loved any task that required repetition and fine motor skills, so layering the potatoes in concentric circles and evenly spreading the cheese delighted her. The bubbling, cheesy finished dish delighted all of us.

I no longer make these well-balanced dinners every night, so my need for a delicious potato dish has diminished. Sam grew up and moved away, the way children do. Grace died suddenly when she was only five, leaving Sam and me to make her Cheesy Potatoes, which we did together, all through his childhood. My youngest child, Annabelle, prefers rice to potatoes anytime. Still, on the nights I roast a chicken, I do make Sam's Potatoes. And on a winter night, Grace's Cheesy Potatoes served with short ribs or thick stews still delight. Just as baked potatoes bring me back to the noisy dinners of my own childhood—the foil and wrinkled skin and hard white flesh—on the nights when I roast or gratin potatoes I am back to that too-small, warm kitchen of my own young family. My children are standing on stools at the counter. Their little hands are layering and sprinkling and tossing potatoes, and for that first bite, I am as happy in the same way as I was back then.

SAM'S POTATOES

These potatoes are best made by a child under the age of ten. Cut the potatoes for him, peel the garlic, and let him do the rest. Tell him that Sam, the boy who invented this, is now twenty-five years old and is an actor living in Brooklyn, New York. He still makes his potatoes regularly.

Serves 4 to 6

INGREDIENTS

Olive oil, enough to coat the bottom of the baking pan and the
    potatoes
4 to 6 potatoes, preferably Yukon Gold, cut into about 8
    chunks apiece
6 to 8 cloves of garlic, peeled
Fresh rosemary
Kosher salt, a small boy's handful
Freshly ground pepper

1. Preheat the oven to 375 degrees F.
2. Drizzle olive oil in a 9-by-12-inch baking dish.
3. Roll the potatoes in the oil so that they are coated.
4. Toss the garlic in.
5. Sprinkle the rosemary leaves around the potatoes.
6. Evenly coat with the salt and pepper.
7. Roll everything around again with your hands.
8. Bake until browned, about 45 minutes.

GRACE'S CHEESY POTATOES

Adapted from *Bistro Cooking*, by Patricia Wells

Bistro Cooking is one of those indispensable cookbooks you should have on hand for whenever you get the urge to go to Paris but can't hop on a plane. My copy is well loved, all stained and dog-eared, mostly because of these potatoes; this recipe is a hybrid of a few au gratin recipes from the book. They taste best when a five-year-old child makes them.

Serves 4 to 6

INGREDIENTS

2 pounds potatoes, peeled and cut as thin as possible (if you
    have a mandolin and, unlike me, aren't terrified to use it,
    this is the time to pull it out of the cupboard; otherwise,
    just do your best with a good paring knife)
1 garlic clove, peeled and halved
1 cup heavy cream
1 cup grated Gruyère cheese (I often splurge on good Gruyère
    for these potatoes because I like them nice and tangy, but
    the regular stuff works just as well)
Kosher salt

1. Preheat the oven to 350 degrees F.
2. Cover the potatoes in water in a saucepan and simmer for about 10 minutes, or until they can easily be pierced with a fork but don't fall apart.

3. Drain.
4. Take the two halves of the garlic clove and vigorously rub the gratin dish (or shallow pan) with the cut side. (This might sound like a step you can skip, but please don't.)
5. Layer half the potatoes in the pan.
6. Add half the cream.
7. Sprinkle with half the cheese.
8. Sprinkle with salt.
9. Repeat: layer half the potatoes on top, and add the rest of the cream and cheese.
10. Sprinkle with salt.
11. Bake uncovered until golden brown and bubbling, about one hour.

Allure

There was a magical period of time when I thought I was happy and living the exact life I should be living. I know that many people feel this way all the time, or at least most of the time. But I had opted for adventures and impulsive decisions for most of my life, and although that meant very high highs, it also meant a fair amount of crashing and burning. No regrets, but I did often feel like I was out of step with other people my age. They were getting married when I was establishing a writing career, having babies when I was getting divorced, sending kids to college when I was having babies.

And then, of course, there were all the losses that kept piling up around me with resounding thuds. My brother, Skip, at thirty from an accident at home. My father at sixty-seven from lung cancer. My five-year-old daughter Grace, suddenly, from a virulent form of strep throat. I always believed in food as the greatest comfort. As Emily Post wrote in her book on etiquette, all you can offer the grieving is a good warm broth. Food can't heal, but it can soothe and comfort us. Sometimes I felt I spent so much time reeling from grief that I couldn't find my balance at all. "Things fall apart," Yeats wrote; "the centre cannot hold."

But there was a brief time when I felt solid, rooted, happy, right.

I lived in a neighborhood in Providence called Fox Point, full of dogwood trees that bloomed pink and white in the spring, and restored Colonial houses, and triple-deckers that sagged under the weight of students from Brown and RISD. I taught creative writing once a week at RISD, walking there along historic Benefit Street, with its gas lamps and landmark buildings, past signer of the Declaration of Independence Stephen Hopkins's house, past Brown University founder John Brown's house, past the Providence Athenaeum (built in 1838) and the First Baptist Church in America (built in 1775), and arriving at my classroom, next door to a room with giant looms and another with knitting machines. The students, painters and furniture makers and sculptors, were all interesting and they were interested in writing, and for their final I had them give a presentation; these often involved videos or blown glass and, once, a young woman playing "Danny Boy" on her violin.

Most days I wrote my novels or articles for magazines like *Good Housekeeping* and *Parenting* and *Redbook*. When I wasn't writing I was taking care of my children, my loves. Sam and Grace. Three years apart. Blond hair and goofy grins. I sliced so many cucumbers and apples. I zipped them into snowsuits and buckled them into rain boots and pulled on mittens and socks. I lay newspaper on the kitchen table and set up finger paints and large sheets of blank white paper. I had them lie on the floor and I traced their beautiful bodies, then cut along the lines and let them dress their shapes up in feathers and glitter. We made clay hot dogs and read books out loud and danced to Beatles songs. I took them to school and picked them up; drove them to swimming and ballet and fencing and art and drama; packed snacks for the car and lunches for school; and I baked cookies every week. I'd sit in the yard and read *The New Yorker* while they rode their bicycles in circles around me.

My friends lived in my neighborhood, in historic houses like mine. There were filmmakers and artists and dancers and writers, and on weekend nights we drank wine and ate expensive cheese, fed our kids quesadillas and put on a video for them to watch while we ate coq au vin or mustard chicken. On one of these nights someone proposed a progressive dinner: appetizers at one house, main course at another, dessert at a third. It felt so grown-up, a progressive dinner. We all seized on the idea and quickly took assignments. There were more neighbors than courses in a dinner, so it was agreed that three couples would take the first one and the other three would be in charge the next time.

I was to do the appetizers. I cannot remember what I made that night, but I do remember the hum of conversation in my dining room, all the children playing in the yard, walking as one large group down Arnold Street to Thayer Street, two blocks away, where the main course would be served in the backyard. Again, I can't remember what we ate, just the memory of one woman taking all the kids to her house across the street to watch a video and the stars hanging heavy over us that summer night and the decision to go and get the dessert and just eat it here in this yard rather than move to the next house. So Mary—she was in charge of dessert—went home and came back with two beautiful peach pies. These were not typical peach pies. They had a shortbread crust and a moist filling and the peaches were ripe and perfect, as only peaches can be at a certain time in summer. In his poem "From Blossoms," Li-Young Lee writes about the pleasure of eating "not only the sugar, but the days." The recipe came from an editor at *Allure* magazine, Mary said. Later, she gave us all copies because we could not stop talking about that pie.

We never did have the second progressive dinner. But the memory of that night—that magical happy time, that pie—has not faded for me, even as the gyre keeps spinning, even as the center doesn't always hold. Not long after that night, Grace died. People moved away, to Santa Fe and New York City. Losses fell upon us all, as they do. We cannot stop them, not even though, as Lee tells us, "There are days we live as if death were nowhere in the background."

Whenever I see peaches in the grocery store, I fill a brown bag with several, knowing that tonight at least, there will be peach pie, a reminder of one magical night when I was, fleetingly, happy.

MARY'S PEACH PIE

I still have this recipe written on paper with the *Allure* logo at the top and LINDA WELLS, EXECUTIVE EDITOR, below the logo. So I can only assume that my friend Mary did indeed get this recipe from Linda Wells. To me, though, it will always be Mary's Peach Pie, served on a magical summer night long ago.

INGREDIENTS

PASTRY

1¼ cups flour

½ teaspoon salt

½ cup cold unsalted butter

2 tablespoons sour cream

FILLING

3 egg yolks

½ cup sugar

2 tablespoons flour

⅓ cup sour cream

3 peaches, peeled and sliced

1. Make the pastry by putting all of the pastry ingredients in a food processor and blending until they just form a ball.

2. Pat into a flat disc, wrap in plastic wrap, and refrigerate for 1 hour.

3. Preheat the oven to 425 degrees F.

4. Pat the chilled dough into a pie tin and bake for 10 minutes.

5. Remove the tin from the oven and reduce the temperature to 350 degrees F. While the piecrust cools, make the filling.

6. Beat the egg yolks lightly and combine with the sugar, flour, and sour cream.

7. Arrange the peach slices on the piecrust.

8. Pour the filling mixture over the peaches and cover with foil.

9. Bake for 35 minutes at 350 degrees F.

10. Remove the foil and bake 10 to 15 more minutes, or until the filling is set.

How to Butcher a Pig

I have been invited to butcher a pig. Matt Gennuso, co-owner and chef of Chez Pascal restaurant in Providence, has come out from the kitchen to my table after a night of gluttony. My then husband and I have eaten mussels and duck confit, steak and chestnut bisque. But what has put me into a state of ecstasy is the pork tasting: house-made sausage, slices of leg, pulled brined shoulder, and a chop. I am a carnivore. And the meat that makes me drool, that makes my heart speed up and my eyes shine, the meat I love the most, is pork.

My moans and sighs have brought Matt into the dining room. Like a tween meeting Justin Timberlake, I gush and giggle and manage to say, "That pork . . ." For a minute, Matt looks as if he isn't sure what to do with me. But then he brightens. "Hey!" he says. "Want to come butcher a pig with me?" "Yes!" I practically shout. I am giddy with pork, giddier with the idea of more pork.

"A lot of people say they'll come and do it," Matt says. "But then they don't."

"No, no," I tell him. "I will come. I want to do it. I want to butcher a pig."

I do not think of blood or Babe. I don't yet think about what it will mean to see exactly where my food comes from. At that moment, I only know that a girl does not get asked to butcher a pig every day.

On the Monday morning I am going to meet Matt, I hurriedly drop my kids off at school, eager to get to the restaurant. I fret about what to wear, unsure of how much blood I might encounter, how much splattering this could involve. Settling on an old button-down shirt and my jeans with the most holes, I remember something a friend told me. On a search for the best authentic jerk pork in Jamaica, he and his wife went to watch a pig being slaughtered. A freshly slaughtered pig, they were told, makes the best jerk pork. His wife has not eaten pork since.

Of course, my pig has been killed several days earlier, in Vermont. I am going to butcher, not to slaughter. Still, I can't help but wonder how squeamish I will be. I am the sort of person who walks quickly past dead squirrels or birds on the sidewalk, looking the other way. However, I love a bloody steak, a juicy lamb chop, and most of all, I love pork in all of its incarnations. One of the highlights of my culinary life was a wedding in North Carolina where we were served a roasted pig complete with its crackling skin. I couldn't get enough.

Among discerning chefs and diners, there is no disputing

that the quality of meat is related to the quality of the animal's life. The rabbit, venison, lamb, and pork that are served at Chez Pascal are all from milk-fed animals who have not had growth hormones or antibiotics. And they are all butchered by Matt.

Many chefs say they butcher their own meat because the act forms an important connection to the source of their food. "Sure," Matt says, "it's easier to have someone else do it. But it doesn't seem right. I just really enjoy it. I love seeing where my food comes from." I did not necessarily have that same belief. Or I hadn't articulated it yet. I did love picking strawberries and eating them still warm from the sun. I always selected local produce and eschewed tomatoes in their tasteless winter form, preferring to wait until they were in season. And I appreciated good food. I sought out restaurants that were innovative, that cooked using locally grown vegetables and naturally raised meats. But did I really need to look my dinner in the eye? When I glanced at that pig's solemn face, would I lose my love of all things pork? Would I be able to thrust a butcher knife, Charles Manson–like, into the animal that had inspired *Charlotte's Web* and the lovable, stuttering Porky Pig?

When I park my car on Hope Street and head toward the kitchen door, I think of my two-year-old daughter, Annabelle, whom we adopted from China a year ago, and the pink face of her most beloved stuffed animal, the eponymously named Piggie. When she asks me, "What did you do today, Mommy?," will I have the courage to actually tell her?

In the kitchen of Chez Pascal, a thirty-five-pound dead pig is lying on a wooden cutting board with four butcher knives glistening beside it. Matt eagerly greets me, ready to get to work. He snaps on surgical gloves and begins to show me where the various cuts of meat come from—loin, ribs, shoulders—moving the stiff pig around as he indicates each section. I try to take notes, but I'm mesmerized by the pig. Its ears stick up straight and look not unlike the kind I buy at Target for my dog, Zuzu, to chew. The gray tongue protrudes from its mouth, and its little pig tail sticks out straight. The pig is a bad shade of yellow, and has been slit open from throat to butt.

"I used to start at the legs and move up," Matt explains. "Now I start at the shoulders and move down. Maybe because I'm left-handed, I do everything backward." He smiles, tosses the pig onto its back, and begins cutting. The bones make funny little crackling noises as they break apart. After Matt dries the cavity and spins the pig around to face me, I peek inside. No blood. But a pair of kidneys are still in there. "People eat these," Matt says. He removes them, and some membrane, and then urges me to feel around until I find the shoulder blades.

Slowly, I grow more comfortable touching the pig. And as Matt expertly removes pieces, he tells me how he will cook them. This will be brined and slow-roasted; this will be marinated. At one point, the pig's head is sitting on its naked neck like something out of a horror movie. But soon enough, Matt removes the head, too.

I begin to understand why Matt does this as he lays out two perfect pork tenderloins. They look exactly like the ones in the meat department of Stop & Shop, except they are fresh. Those supermarket tenderloins in their tight plastic wrappings have been around a long time.

The pig is starting to look less and less like anything recognizable, and I am starting to get used to the sound of bones breaking. Matt uses his fingers as much as he uses a knife, or even more. The meat comes off easily. "Let the knife and the meat do what they want to do," Matt says. Here are the ribs, looking exactly like ribs. And the hip, with its ball and socket. "Some people see the whole animal and they think, *Oh, poor pig!*" he says. "But he wasn't somebody's pet. He was raised for this."

I am surprised that this thought—*Oh, poor pig!*—does not come into my own mind. Instead, I am standing here while the pig is being butchered, and I am feeling a mixture of awe and gratitude. Matt tells me he likes to come in here alone in the morning to do the butchering, and I understand why.

There is almost a reverence about the process. When Matt cleans the table of bone and pig parts and puts the meat together like a 3-D jigsaw puzzle of pork, I am amazed. I am impressed. And unlike my friend's wife, I am hungry. Hungry for the bacon Matt will smoke, and the loin he will marinate with lemon zest, fennel seed, parsley, crushed red pepper, Dijon mustard, and olive oil. Hungry for the sausages. Hungry, still, for pork in all its delicious forms.

Weeks after I butcher the pig with Matt, I am eating at a

fancy restaurant in New York City with friends. The special
that night is roast suckling pig. I ask the waiter if it is milk-
fed, from a sustainable farm. It is. And I order it, happily and
eagerly. As I eat, I have the same thought I had that morning
at Chez Pascal as Matt offered up the beautiful natural pork:
As Charlotte said of Wilbur, "That's some pig."

MATT GENNUSO'S CASSOULET

Cassoulet of Pork Sausage, Duck Confit,
Flageolet Beans and Herbed Bread Crumbs

The first time I had cassoulet, that meaty, beany, slow-
cooked dish from the south of France, was at a now-defunct
restaurant called Quatorze, on West Fourteenth Street. I still
always order it at Café Luxembourg—or, really, anywhere I
see it on the menu. The one at Chez Pascal is transcendent,
and if you find yourself in Providence, Rhode Island, go
straight there and hope that it is available. If it isn't, you will
still have a transcendent meal, of course. Matt and his wife,
Kristin, have shared Matt's recipe, so that when you are not
in Providence on a cold fall or winter weekend and crave cassoulet, you can make it yourself. It takes a little planning and
a few days, which is why it's a perfect weekend recipe. Cassoulet is a gastronomical commitment. And a worthy one.
Your friends will be impressed. And you will feel accom-
plished, and satisfied.

Serves 4

Please note that this is a three-day process.

Day 1:
   1 cup flageolet beans
   4 cups water

1. Soak the flageolet beans in the water overnight, uncovered in the refrigerator.

Day 2:
   3 tablespoons blended oil for cooking; olive oil is also fine
   2 pounds pork stew meat, cut into ½-inch cubes
   2 cups carrots, diced into large pieces
   2 cups diced onions
   2 tablespoons minced garlic
   ½ cup white wine
   3 cups veal or beef stock
   3 cups chicken stock
   1½ teaspoons quatre épices
   2 bay leaves

1. Preheat the oven to 350 degrees F.
2. In a large ovenproof rondeau pan or deep stockpot, over medium-high heat, add enough cooking oil to coat the bottom of the pan. Once the oil just begins to smoke, carefully place the pork, a little at a time, into the pan. You want to sear the meat, not stew it. If you place too much meat into

the pan, it will cool down and the meat will sweat, not sear. You are not cooking the pork through at this point, just lightly browning it. Once the pork has taken on a golden-brown color, remove it from the pan and set it aside.

3. Discard the cooking oil and the grease that has come from the meat. Pour a dash of new cooking oil into the pan, enough to coat the bottom, and add the diced carrots and onions. Cook for 4 to 6 minutes. Add the garlic and cook till you can smell its aroma. Deglaze the pan with the white wine and cook until half the liquid evaporates. Add the veal or beef stock and the chicken stock and bring to a boil. Then add the quatre épices, bay leaves, flageolet beans, and your reserved seared pork and place the pan in the oven. Cook, uncovered, at 350 degrees F for 2 to 3 hours, stirring every 30 minutes or so. During this stage, you are developing color and flavor. As the stew is cooking, a "skin" or flor (a term from the wine world) is developing on top of it. It is important to stir the stew in order to mix that skin back into the base of the stew. If left unattended, the stew can burn, and that will impart an unpleasant taste. So stir your stew.

4. Once cooked, the beans and the pork should be very tender. Season with salt and pepper to taste. This is your cassoulet base, or stew base. Let cool and place in the refrigerator overnight.

Day 3:

> *2 pounds pork sausage, precooked, cut into fourths or thirds,*
>   *crosswise*
> *4 duck confit legs, skin removed*
> *Herbed bread crumbs*

NOTE: You'll need 4 ovenproof dishes for serving the cassoulet.

1. Preheat the oven to 400 degrees F.
2. In the four ovenproof dishes, evenly distribute the cassoulet base you made the day before and the precooked sausage; the cassoulet base goes in first, with the sausage on top. Place the duck confit legs in the center of each dish.
3. Bake at 400 degrees F for fifteen to twenty minutes, or until the broth has reduced and is bubbling and thick. Sprinkle the herbed bread crumbs on top, continue cooking for four to five minutes, until the bread crumbs are browned, and serve.

Risi e Bisi

When we adopted our daughter Annabelle from Hunan, China, in 2005, she had been fed only baby formula for the six months she'd lived at the orphanage in Loudi. We cannot say what nourishment she'd had for her first five months, before she arrived early on a September morning at the door of the orphanage, tucked into a cardboard box and dressed all in blue and white—socks, pants, shirt. At the orphanage, they named her Lou Fu Jing. *Lou* because all the baby girls at that orphanage were named for the city of Loudi, as if that gave them a place to be from, a homeland, a history. *Fu* for good luck, a way to counter these abandoned daughters' bad luck in their short lives. Each baby got her own third name—actually the first name in the Chinese order of reading names—one that suited or described them. *Jing* means bright, like a light; she was given that name because, they said, she brightened a room. With her wide and easy toothless smile, her black hair sticking up all over her head, and a mischievous twinkle in her eyes, the name suited her perfectly.

For my then husband and our son, Sam, and me, she did more than brighten the room in the city office building where we first held her in our arms and the rooms in the cities across China we traveled to that chilly March week to sign papers and more papers to finalize the adoption. Annabelle brightened our lives, which had darkened since we'd lost Grace over two years earlier. Although we had returned to home-cooked dinners and weekend trips in our VW van and boisterous games of cards or Clue, a gloom still hung over us, a grief that, although almost imperceptible to the outside world, still lingered in our home and hearts. Annabelle, that bright light, brought us joy and hope and even optimism again.

We arrived in China with a bag packed with things from a checklist the orphanage had sent out: baby clothes and toys and stuffed animals, antibiotics and scabies medication, and two weeks' worth of baby bottles and nipples. On the bus less than thirty minutes after we were handed Annabelle, our guide took the microphone to address the ten stunned families with new daughters on their laps. She held up a baby bottle and said, "First thing, snip off tip of nipple. This formula very, very thick." Cans of thick, sandlike formula were distributed; nipples were snipped; the ratio of formula to water was given. The result was a swampy mortar that required hard sucking, even with that wider opening in the nipple. "Don't change the formula until you get home," the doctor traveling with us warned. "But by all means, feed these babies. They're hungry."

Feed we did.

Annabelle ate wok-fried shrimp, soup dumplings, cold noodles; eggs, pancakes, waffles, omelets; lychees, pineapple, pears, watermelon, cantaloupe, strawberries; octopus, congee, fried rice. In other words, she ate everything we gave her, happily slurping and chewing and sucking. Until we got home and suddenly almost everything was sniffed, touched, and rejected. A little avocado, a dollop of hummus, an egg if the yolk wasn't runny, plain pasta with butter, fruit and sometimes carrots or mashed potatoes. "Can a kid live on this diet?" I asked our pediatrician. My other kids had eaten anything and everything. "It all evens out," he said. "One day all watermelon, the next all pasta."

Eventually her refrain at dinner became "No sauce!" "Too crunchy!" "There's pepper on this! I see black dots!" "Too spicy!" "Too mushy!" "Too gross!"

Slowly I learned what she liked, and tried to rotate her four favorite (by this I mean *only*) meals. Other mothers looked at me with pity as I ordered Annabelle plain pasta with just butter, and cheese *on the side*. They bragged about how their kids loved duck confit, capers, caviar. Internally I screamed, *I had kids like that once too!* Instead, I cut off the crusts on her grilled cheese sandwiches, removed the fries that were too crispy, made sure the eggs didn't touch the bacon.

Then one night, I came home from a long, long day; I had taught in New York City the night before, held office hours for students in the morning, met an editor for lunch, then raced for a train back home in time to make dinner for Annabelle and me. When I opened the pantry door, I saw that its shelves were woefully bare. Too rushed to go grocery shopping, I'd banked on our usual supply of boxes of pasta and a can or two of Campbell's chicken and stars soup. The freezer held only ice cream, jars of pesto and vodka sauce—useless without pasta—and . . . well . . . ice. No, wait. Behind the ice cream sat a bag of frozen peas.

Even Annabelle liked peas, usually with chicken or pork chops, both of which we did not have. But back in the pantry I'd seen a bag of arborio rice and neat boxes of chicken broth. Rice. Chicken broth. Peas. That combination meant one thing to me: *Risi e Bisi*, or rice and peas Italian-style.

I did not grow up eating risotto. That is a northern Italian dish, cooked in a broth to a creamy consistency, made with a short-grained rice like arborio. But over my years of teaching myself to cook, it had become one of the dishes I'd grown to love to make and to eat. I made mushroom risotto, soaking dried porcinis and adding them to a mix of other mushrooms, with the soaking liquid added to the broth. I made tomato risotto and sausage and rapini risotto and even bacon risotto. People are afraid to try making risotto because it takes time and care—the very reasons I love to cook it.

I had shallots that night, though onion would do, too. I had Parmesan cheese—essential to a good risotto—and

butter, also essential. Like knitting or reading, slowly adding simmering broth, a third cup at a time, to the rice and
stirring is calming, even meditative. The heat must not be
too high, the broth must not be added too quickly, the cook
must be patient. Stirring risotto is highly recommended
when you've just gotten off Amtrak after less than twenty-
four hours in Manhattan. It's highly recommended when you
are so tired you can't even dial for pizza delivery. It's highly
recommended when you have a daughter who does not want
food that is too spicy, too crispy, too mushy, too peppery, too
saucy. The rice is firm to the tooth. The broth is creamy. The
flavorings are subtle.

When the rice was perfect, I added the Parmesan and a
tablespoon of butter, stirred, and put some in my favorite
bright blue bowl. Annabelle eyed it suspiciously. But by now
I was calm and hungry, having found the Zen of making
risotto.

"You're going to like it," I told her.

"What are the green things?"

"Peas."

She sniffed. She poked. She tasted.

"Hmmm," she said.

I waited.

"More," my picky eater said.

Annabelle's Risi e Bisi

Italian Rice and Peas

This is actually a recipe for risotto, and once you learn the basic steps of making a good risotto, you can go crazy with it: Soak dried porcini for 15 minutes, chop them up along with other assorted mushrooms, and then do everything as listed here, except instead of adding peas, add the mushrooms. Or cook Italian sausage and add it, with some cremini mushrooms, instead of the peas. Or make this recipe but also add cooked chopped bacon along with the peas. The secret is to not rush the cooking. Just keep ladling ⅓ cup of warm chicken broth to the rice, each time stirring until it's all absorbed before you add more. I think the final tablespoon of butter at the very end does something magical to the risotto, but sometimes so eager have I been to eat my *Risi e Bisi* that I've forgotten it, and no one has even noticed.

Serves 3 or 4

INGREDIENTS

1 quart chicken broth

2 tablespoons olive oil

1 shallot, chopped

1 cup arborio rice

1 cup frozen peas

Salt and pepper

½ cup grated Parmesan, plus more for serving

1 tablespoon unsalted butter

1. Warm the chicken broth in a saucepan, keeping it just below a simmer.
2. Heat the olive oil in a deep skillet. (I like to make risotto in my orange Le Creuset Dutch oven.)
3. Sauté the chopped shallot for about a minute.
4. Add the arborio rice and stir it around, toasting it, for a minute or two.
5. Begin to ladle the chicken broth, ⅓ cup at a time, into the rice, stirring with each addition until the broth is absorbed.
6. Keep adding and stirring until the rice is al dente and creamy, about 20 to 25 minutes.
7. Stir in the peas.
8. Take the pan off the heat and add the salt, pepper, and Parmesan cheese.
9. Add the butter and give the rice a good stir.
10. Serve with more grated cheese on the side.

Five Ways of Looking at the Tomato

I

"The nation is in chaos. Can nothing stop this tomato onslaught?" asks a character in the 1978 movie *Attack of the Killer Tomatoes*. In the movie, mutant tomatoes are killing people and pets, and several scientists band together to stop them. A silly idea, and a bad movie ("Not even worthy of sarcasm," one reviewer wrote), but the tomato has suffered from a bad reputation throughout history. In fact, in the 1700s, the tomato was called the "poison apple," and Europeans actually feared it because aristocrats got sick and died after eating tomatoes. Or so people thought. Actually, the aristocrats ate off pewter plates, and the high acidity of the tomato leached lead from the plates; the rich were dying not from the tomato but from lead poisoning.

The tomato's origins go back to the Aztecs, who ate them

way back in A.D. 700. We have the Spanish conquistador Hernán Cortés to thank for bringing tomato seeds to Europe in the early 1500s, not to eat but for decorative purposes. Perhaps because my grandparents' home city of Naples, Italy, changed the tomato's reputation in 1880 by inventing pizza and, therefore, popularizing the dreaded deadly nightshade, I have always had a love affair with the tomato. "Star of earth," Pablo Neruda calls it in "Ode to Tomatoes," and, indeed, when I remember the tomatoes of my youth, warm from the sun in my grandmother's yard, that description is apt. Nonna, my great-grandmother, would pick one, wipe the dirt off on her faded apron, and give it to me to eat just like that, the pulp and juice dribbling down my chin when I bit into it.

The tomato takes front and center in southern Italian households like mine because our elixir is tomato sauce. That was my after-school snack on the days Mama Rose made her huge pot of gravy (as we referred to spaghetti sauce), poured onto crusty bread and slurped down. And it appeared not just on bread or spaghetti but in parmigianas—eggplant, chicken, veal—lasagna, gnocchi, polenta, cacciatore, pizzaiola, and even on fried eggs. Jars of gravy lined the freezer shelves, and when I grew up and moved away, emergency supplies of it were brought to Boston and New York and even packed into my luggage and checked through to St. Louis.

II

Of course tomatoes appeared in the BLTs of my youth, and on the sandwiches we ate for Saturday lunch, when Mama Rose would spread a cornucopia of salumi across the kitchen table, accompanied by cheeses—two kinds of provolone and, oddly, American—and hard rolls and lettuce and sliced tomatoes. They appeared in the salads that accompanied dinner, always iceberg lettuce with sliced cucumbers and wedges of tomatoes (pale and mushy in winter, sold in a three-pack wrapped in cellophane) drenched with oil and red wine vinegar.

But it was when I was an adult that my relationship with the tomato really took off. And that began with my friend Matt. Matt lives in Los Angeles, and when I visited there he made me the most simple dinner, one that I have copied and tweaked ever since. He diced ripe tomatoes and riper Brie, tossed them with hot pasta, and topped it all with sliced fresh basil. When it is hot and humid here on the East Coast, I often make some version of Matt's dish. Only the pasta needs to be cooked—no oven or standing over a hot stove—and it can feed a crowd easily. Now that the Brie craze of the 1980s has passed, I usually substitute fresh mozzarella. But the result is the same gooey, cheesy, tomatoey deliciousness.

III

Around the same time—the 1980s—I had my first caprese
salad, that simple combination of fresh tomatoes and sliced
mozzarella drizzled with olive oil and sprinkled with basil.
Yes, I know that this salad is ubiquitous now, on every menu
at every restaurant everywhere. But the first time I tasted one,
I swooned at its astounding simplicity. Looking back, I think
that this is the moment when I understood that using the simplest, best ingredients produces the best food—better than
the overcomplicated dishes I labored over in my early cooking days: a heavily breaded chicken Kiev, stuffed with butter
and rolled in a mixture of dry herbs, or chicken-fried steak
with white gravy. Here were basically two ingredients—
tomato and mozzarella—changing the way I thought.

Apparently, when my maternal grandfather sat down to
supper, he would look at the food spread before him and ask
rhetorically, "Do you know how much this would cost in a
restaurant?" The point being that eating at home cost far
less than eating out—and the food was better. That caprese
salad in that Manhattan restaurant brought my grandfather's
question to mind. When I read the description on the menu
and saw the price, I knew I would never order such a thing.
A few tomatoes and a ball of mozzarella from the grocery
store cost far less. Lucky for me, someone else at the table
did order it, and I realized that, in fact, sometimes even
though a meal costs more at a restaurant, that perfect olive

oil, that perfect mozzarella, those ripe tomatoes are worth every penny. Of course, now I splurge on the best ingredients, and I make caprese salads whenever I can get tomatoes that don't look like the ones from Mama Rose's winter dinner salads.

IV

One of the twists I make on a caprese salad is to use sliced cherry tomatoes and serve them with mozzarella on a bed of arugula. As much as I love the tomato, I also love the cherry tomato. "Handful of skinned sunsets," Sandra Beasley calls them in her poem "Cherry Tomatoes." As with all first loves, I remember the precise moment I fell for these. I was at the Virginia Festival of the Book, in Charlottesville, and my friend Jill threw a party for some of us writers. There was lots of wine and lots of friends and such good cheer in that room that I suppose the party would have been a success even if Jill hadn't served cold sliced tenderloin with roasted cherry tomatoes topped with feta, all of it ready to be piled onto toasted sourdough or scooped up with our greedy fingers. But to me, that evening was made even more memorable because of that food Jill made, and I have roasted cherry tomatoes ever since for parties. Okay, not just for parties. Right now, as I am writing this, I have a half sheet pan of cherry tomatoes roasting in a 180 degree oven for my own lunch. I will let them cool and toss them with arugula and leftover sweet corn scraped from the cob. "Blood of a perfect household," Beasley writes.

V

My final word on tomatoes, at least for now, is that just last summer my son, Sam, was in a play at the Fringe Festival in Edinburgh, Scotland, and his friend James, who wrote and also acted in that play (shameless plug: you can follow their theater company, What Will the Neighbors Say?, on Facebook), is from Glasgow, and James's parents threw a closing party for them. Annabelle and my cousin and I took the lovely train from Edinburgh to Glasgow, and made our way to the Clementses' house, where wine was being poured and food was laid out gloriously on a table on a sunlit patio.

It should come as no surprise that I made a beeline for a platter of cherry tomatoes, arranged beside a small bowl of sea salt. I assumed, correctly, that the idea was to roll the tomato in the salt and pop it into my mouth. Which I did, expecting that eruption Beasley describes so perfectly in her poem. But the eruption I got was even more delicious, not just because of the salt. "What is in this tomato?" I asked James's mother, Kirsty. "Vodka!" she said. Yes! That was what made this eruption so spectacular: the tomatoes were like miniature, chewable Bloody Marys! Kirsty explained the process, which was simply pouring a bottle of vodka over cherry tomatoes and letting them sit overnight. The vodka, she told me, infused with tomato, made a spectacular Bloody Mary.

The tomato has come a long way from its bad reputation as a poison apple. The USDA tells us that over fifteen million tons of tomatoes are produced here every year, 94 percent of them in California. Mostly we consume tomatoes in sauce, like I did growing up and still do when I go to my mother's for dinner. It's the fourth most popular vegetable, after the potato, the onion, and lettuce.

They are waiting for me now, roasted, plump, juicy. Lunch.

GOGO'S SAUCE

It is perfectly acceptable, if not preferable, to call this *gravy* instead of *sauce*. Make it by the gallon and freeze it so you always have some on hand. This recipe will make enough gravy for 3 or 4 pasta dinners, or a combination of pasta and Parmesans.

INGREDIENTS

The oil you saved from making "Gogo's Meatballs" (page 30)
    and "Gloria and Hood's Sausage and Peppers" (page 82)
1 small onion, sliced thin

3 to 4 cloves garlic, peeled and diced

Salt and pepper

Crushed red pepper flakes

¼ cup Italian parsley, chopped

2 cups red wine

4 cans of tomato paste (Gogo uses only Hunt's)

One 28-ounce can chopped tomatoes (again, she uses Hunt's,
but substituting San Marzano tomatoes wouldn't hurt)

One 28-ounce can tomato puree (ditto)

1 tablespoon sugar

1. Heat the oil and sauté the onion until soft and translucent.
2. Sauté the garlic.
3. Add salt, pepper, red pepper flakes, and parsley.
4. Add the wine and be sure to deglaze the pan.
5. Add the tomato paste, stirring as you do so.
6. Add the chopped tomatoes and the puree.
7. Add the sugar.
8. Fill the empty 28-ounce cans with water, and add some to the sauce if it's too thick.
9. Simmer for 3½ to 4 hours.
10. As the sauce simmers, turn it from time to time!

MATT'S PASTA WITH TOMATOES AND BRIE

I make this only in summer when tomatoes are fresh and ripe, though if you are not as particular a tomato person as I am, it's delicious year-round. Below is a tweaked version of Matt's recipe, but I often substitute mozzarella for the Brie. Any melty cheese should work.

Serves 4

INGREDIENTS

A couple pints of cherry tomatoes or 4 or 5 plum tomatoes,
  halved
Olive oil
Salt and pepper
1 pound short pasta such as rigatoni
A small wedge of Brie, the size it comes in at your grocery
  store in that little round box
A handful of fresh basil, chopped

1. Halve the tomatoes and place in a pretty pasta bowl with a good drizzle of olive oil; season with salt and pepper. Let them sit at room temperature.
2. Boil salted water and cook the pasta until it's al dente. Be sure to reserve about ¼ cup of the cooking liquid.
3. While the pasta is cooking, dice the cheese and distribute it on top of the tomatoes.

4. Pour the hot drained pasta into the bowl with the tomatoes and cheese and toss, being sure to get that cheese
   melty. Add the reserved cooking water to help with this
   if necessary.
5. Top with the basil and again season with salt and pepper.

BETTER THAN A RESTAURANT
CAPRESE SALAD

Honestly, after making this at home, I don't even order it in
restaurants anymore—unless I'm in Italy and can't resist the
gorgeous tomatoes and fresh buffalo mozzarella. I like to mix
up the sizes, shapes, and colors of the tomatoes. Although
you can serve this as a salad, it also makes a delicious vegetarian sandwich: just put it in a good Italian roll with a little
olive oil.

Serves 4 to 6

INGREDIENTS

Arugula
About 2 pounds of fresh tomatoes—cherry, plum, heirloom,
   large or small ones—halved or sliced, depending on size
Good olive oil
Salt and pepper
1 ball fresh mozzarella, sliced

1 ball smoked mozzarella, sliced
A splash of balsamic vinegar
A handful of chopped basil

1. Make a bed of arugula on your favorite platter.
2. Place the tomatoes on top and drizzle with olive oil, then season with salt and pepper.
3. Layer on the sliced cheeses so that you basically have a tomato-cheese pattern.
4. Drizzle more olive oil and a splash of balsamic vinegar, and again season with salt and pepper.
5. Sprinkle the basil over everything.

Variation

Add sliced prosciutto di Parma to your pattern: tomato, cheese, prosciutto.

Another Variation

Drizzle pesto sauce on top, in place of the olive oil and basil. Pesto is so easy to make that I just whip it up in my food processor. You can too; if you don't have lots of fresh basil on hand, you can use store-bought. Or just wait until summer.

INGREDIENTS

2 cups fresh basil
3 garlic cloves, peeled
1 cup pecans

1 cup olive oil
1½ cups of either Parmesan or Romano, or a mix of the two
A big pinch of salt
Freshly ground black pepper

1. Chop the basil, garlic, and pecans in a food processor.
2. With the motor running, add the olive oil in a steady stream.
3. Pour the mixture into a bowl and stir in the cheese and salt and pepper.
4. Taste and adjust the seasonings.
5. Drizzle over the caprese salad.
6. Put any leftover pesto in a mason jar and either freeze it, so that you can have a little bit of summer next winter, or use it on pasta tomorrow night.

JILL'S TENDERLOIN AND ROASTED TOMATOES

Anytime I see Jill, which isn't often enough, I ask her to make both dishes. The last time was at her home in Wilmington, North Carolina, and they were as good as I'd remembered. When I asked her for the recipes, she said, "Both are so simple!" They are. And they make an elegant, unforgettable cocktail party dish.

Serves 6 to 8

For the tenderloin:

INGREDIENTS

Salt and pepper

3 to 4 cloves garlic, crushed

One 2- to 3-pound tenderloin, with the ends cut off and
*   saved for some other dish, so that you just have a big*
*   center cut*

1. Preheat the oven to 450 degrees F.
2. Make a paste with salt, pepper, and the garlic and spread
   it nice and thick all over the meat.
3. Roast at 450 degrees for twenty minutes.
4. Turn the oven down to 350 degrees and finish cooking.
   (Figure on about 10 to 15 minutes per pound.)
5. Let the meat rest.
6. Slice.
7. From Jill: "Simple, right?"

For the tomatoes:

INGREDIENTS

18 to 20 Roma tomatoes, cut in half; smaller ones work best

Olive oil

Sea salt

Pepper

Sugar

Feta, sliced mozzarella, or a few shaves of good parmesan

1. Preheat the oven to 250 degrees F.
2. Place the tomatoes on a baking sheet lined with parchment.
3. Drizzle a little olive oil over them.
4. Sprinkle with sea salt, pepper, and a tiny bit of sugar.
5. Bake for 2 to 2½ hours, until they are dried out.
6. Serve at room temperature with the cheese mixed in.

NOTE: I'm a big fan of feta with these, though you can try it every which way. Also, I add some sprigs of thyme to the tomatoes before I roast them.

KIRSTY WARK'S BLOODY MARY TOMATOES

The night before your cocktail party, pour a bottle of vodka over 2 or 3 pints of scored cherry tomatoes. The next evening, drain them and put them in a serving bowl, on a platter, with a ramekin of sea salt, a ramekin of coarsely ground pepper, and a ramekin of celery salt for rolling the tomatoes in. Use the tomato-infused vodka for Bloody Marys the next morning.

How to Smoke Salmon

My son, Sam, and I stand side by side in our tiny back-yard in Providence, shivering. It's late afternoon on New Year's Eve, the sky a battleship gray and snowflakes falling furiously around us. I have to squint up all six feet, five inches of Sam when I talk to him. At seventeen, although he is man-sized, he still has a round baby face and the final hurrah of blond in his darkening hair.

"Do we just stand here?" I ask Sam.

"We have to tend it," he says.

It is the smoker I got for Christmas, and Sam and I are smoking all kinds of pork—loin, ribs, chops—for a New Year's Eve supper. When I watched him start to put the smoker together, with the instructions still in the box, I couldn't help but remember all the Transformers and Legos he used to construct without ever referring to the directions.

Some things never change, I think as he adjusts air vents and reads the temperature dials. And other things, I think with a pang in my heart, change a lot. Like: the piles of college applications on the desk upstairs, the SAT study guide beside Sam's bed, the schedule of auditions hanging on the kitchen bulletin board.

Soon, theater programs around the country will be sending Sam their decisions. Which means that in the not-so-distant future, Sam will go away to college in Pittsburgh or Chicago or Ithaca. I swear, yesterday he had to stand on a stool to layer the sliced apples in the pan for Apple Crisp. I used to lift him into the grocery cart with one swoop, and teach him how to choose a ripe avocado.

Now he regularly makes polenta for dinner, bakes bûche de Noël, feeds us almost daily.

"Needs more water," Sam announces. He is blurry in the snow, moving back inside to refill the jug.

Eleven hours. That's how long it took for that meat to smoke perfectly. At a certain point, I went back into the house, to the warmth of the fire in the kitchen fireplace. But Sam stayed out there, the snow becoming an official blizzard, the wind increasing. He learned how to use that smoker that night, and for months afterward he smoked clams and oysters, tomatoes and garlic for salsa, briskets and more ribs.

Spring came, and with it those college acceptances. I watched Sam's face light up whenever an e-mail dropped into his box with good news. He had wanted to be an actor since

he was eight, and now he was on his way to a BFA program
six hours from our home in Providence. For his own going-
away party, Sam smoked pork tenderloins. I looked out the
kitchen window at him tending the smoker. It was a mystery to me how it worked; I just let Sam be the smoke master.
Around me, his half-packed duffel bags lay on the floor. A
box of books. Linens for his dorm room bed. The next day,
with our bellies full, we drove him to college.

The sadness that comes from your first child leaving home
is, of course, not the saddest thing of all. But the ache, the
sense that something is missing, the way you keep looking up,
expecting him to burst through the door in his size 13 shoes—
that is real. In an instant, family dinner changes, shrinks,
quiets considerably. The smoker sits, alone and untended,
amid the falling leaves. Then another winter, another snowstorm. But this time the smoker remains unused, half-hidden
by snow.

Oh, Sam comes home, a whirling dervish of laundry and
anecdotes about college and dates to see old friends.

"Maybe we could smoke some ribs?" I suggest, like a girl
asking a boy to a prom.

"Great idea," Sam says as he runs out the door to meet up
with someone from high school.

"You hardly ever saw that kid when you went to school
with him," I grumble. But Sam doesn't hear me. He's a blur
of denim disappearing around the corner.

The smoker and I endure a lonely spring, the azaleas blooming fuchsia around us as I stand side by side with the smoker in the yard, missing Sam. But I imagine a summer of smoked pork and seafood. A summer of Sam home.

"I got cast with the Missoula Children's Theatre!" Sam shouts into the phone across the three hundred miles that separate us.

"Missoula?" I gulp. "Montana?"

"I start Memorial Day," he says, and he is so excited that all I can do is be happy for him.

July. Sam is not home, as I had imagined; he is out west, touring in *Cinderella*. Sometimes he sends me pictures of him hamming for the camera. The baby fat is gone. His face is all angles and planes now. There is the shadow of a beard across his cheeks and chin. I show the pictures to my friends Mark and Heather. We are on their roof deck in Portland, Oregon, nibbling cheese and olives and fruit and smoked salmon that Mark smoked himself the day before.

"That's Sam?" Heather says, her blue eyes wide. "I remember when he was only this tall."

"So do I," I say, staring down at the photo of the young man who is my son. Four and a half pounds when he was born, so tiny he fit in his father's hand. I can still feel him pressed against me in his Snugli, my stalwart companion.

The smoky-sweet flavor of the salmon fills my mouth, and I think of my own smoker, abandoned in the backyard. I realize that I have felt abandoned too, by Sam, by all the years racing past. But here I am on a beautiful summer day, eating

with friends. I have raised a happy kid and he hasn't abandoned me; he's simply growing up.

"How did you make this?" I ask Mark.

He gives me his recipe, but I'm only half-listening. My
mind is back in Providence, finding those never-read instructions and stoking up that smoker, learning how to monitor
the temperature, when to add water, how to adjust the vents
to allow the smoke to stay alive.

And that is what I do when I get back home. I unearth the
directions and read them carefully. Then I light the coals, fill
the bottom with water, lay the salmon that I've brined for two
days on top of the grill, and cover it all. Smoke escapes from
beneath the lid. *It's working*, I marvel. I stand there under
the hot July sun and tend the smoker. Like most things in
life, smoking salmon requires your attention. It takes time
and care. When I lift the lid, a perfect piece of pink smoked
salmon waits for me. Unexpectedly, my eyes tear up.

That night I tell Sam over the phone how I smoked salmon.

"The fire went out too fast," I admit.

"You probably cut the oxygen off by closing the vents,"
he says.

"I'll remember that for next time," I say.

"I've got to go," Sam says. "I love you, Mom."

Before I can answer him, he's gone, on his way to his big,
bright future. Out the window, the last of the smoke floats
above the sunflowers, into the blue summer sky. I open the
recipe book that came with the smoker, the one Sam never

took out of the box. Chicken. Trout. Beef tenderloin. I will try them all, I decide. I will savor every bit.

SMOKED SALMON INSPIRED BY
MARK AND HEATHER

INGREDIENTS

1 cup kosher salt

½ cup white sugar

½ cup brown sugar

2 tablespoons crushed black peppercorns

Two 2-pound salmon fillets or sides, pin bones removed

Olive oil

Salt

Pepper

Lemon

Orange marmalade

Cucumbers, sour cream, capers, small toasts

1. Assemble the smoker according to its directions—unless, like Sam, you know how to do it without reading them. Cedar or alderwood chips work best with salmon.
2. *Two days before you plan to smoke the salmon, make a dry brine.* In a bowl, mix together the salt, sugar, brown sugar, and peppercorns. Roll out a sheet of extra-wide aluminum foil a little longer than the length of the fish and top with

an equally long layer of plastic wrap. Sprinkle ⅓ of the rub on the plastic. Lay one filet on the rub, skin side down. Sprinkle ⅓ of the rub over the flesh side of the salmon. Place the second salmon fillet, flesh side down, on the first fillet. Use the remaining rub to cover the skin on the top piece. Fold the plastic over to cover, then close the edges of foil together and crimp tightly around the fish.

3. Place the wrapped fish on a plank or sheet pan and top with another plank or pan. Weight with a heavy phone book or a brick or two and refrigerate for 12 to 24 hours. Flip the fish over and refrigerate for another 12 hours. Some juice will leak out during the process, so make sure there's a place for the runoff to gather.

4. Unwrap the fish and rinse off the cure with cold water. Pat the salmon with paper towels, then place in a cool, dry place (not the refrigerator) until the surface of the fish is dry and matte-like; this will take 1 to 3 hours, depending on the humidity. A fan may be used to speed the process.

5. Place each fillet on foil. Brush with olive oil and season with salt and pepper to taste, then add a squirt of lemon juice.

6. Smoke the fish over smoldering hardwood chips or sawdust, keeping the temperature inside the smoker between 150 degrees and 160 degrees F until the thickest part of the fish registers 150 degrees, about 20 minutes.

7. Let cool. Spread a light glaze of good orange marmalade on each fillet (this is what made my friend Mark's so yummy), then serve with cucumber rounds, sour cream, capers, and small toasts.

The Summer of Omelets

Annabelle wants to learn how to make an omelet. She is twelve, and suspicious of most food. A few years ago, my mother taught her to make scrambled eggs, which is the only way Annabelle will have eggs. Except for hard-boiled, but then she removes the hard yolk and eats only the white part, with salt. Egg yolks are high on her list of things that are too disgusting to eat. When she eats berries, which she loves, she examines each one and sets aside any that are discolored, bruised, too soft, or too hard.

When eating changed for her, I cannot pinpoint. At a birthday party when she was two, she sat primly to the side, delicately nibbling capers one by one. Next thing I knew, she liked only white food: pasta, chicken, rice, the white part of eggs. But the summer of the omelets, Annabelle and I are gypsies, living together in borrowed apartments and condos,

B and Bs, and Airbnbs, across two continents. Her father and I are getting divorced, and housing is an issue. For reasons that have nothing to do with omelets, he is staying in the house where our family has lived for seventeen years, a 1792 red Colonial with a bright blue door where I raised my babies, and mourned the death of my daughter Grace, and wrote my books, and learned to knit. There is still glitter from Grace's art projects in the cracks of the floorboards. Our dog Zuzu, now fifteen, has stained the kitchen floor with her worn-out bladder. The closet has pencil lines marking the growth of the kids. That house is, as Neruda said, "the shore of the heart where I have roots." Leaving is hard; we know this. Leaving these fingerprints of a lifetime harder.

But Annabelle and I have found a loft across the city, with soaring ceilings and big silver pipes and windows that let more sunlight than a person knows what to do with stream in. The only catch is securing a mortgage. Self-employed people are precarious financial risks, apparently. I spend a good part of this nomadic summer scanning documents—bank, car loan, retirement—and signing papers and writing letters about why I paid my Target credit card bill late in March 2011 and why I teach only sometimes and where exactly do I get the money my tax returns say I get. It's exhausting, this scanning and signing, this packing of suitcases every week and lugging bags through lobbies and up stairs and in and out of the trunk of my Fiat. This summer of endings and new beginnings, it's exhausting.

Every morning, in whatever kitchen I find myself in, I make Annabelle breakfast. Pancakes with a side of perfect raspberries. Toad in a hole with sliced strawberries (on their own plate, to be sure that the red of the strawberries does not touch the white of the egg or the toast). Once, chicken and stars soup, a dare to see if I would give her soup for breakfast. Once, a fat wedge of watermelon eaten straight off the rind. But the morning I make myself a ham and Swiss omelet, Annabelle studies me as I move through the steps—the beating of the eggs with a fork as butter waltzes in a frying pan, the way I gently lift the cooked egg to let the uncooked slide beneath it. "Teach me," she says. "I want to make you an omelet every morning, and bring it to you in bed."

I recognize this need to care for me. All summer she's been watching me for signs of distress. As Annabelle sorts out this new life we're embarking on, she's wondering how I will be in it, despite my promises that we will all be okay. Some mornings she jumps up, all bedhead and half-closed eyes, to make me coffee. One night when I complained I was hungry, she ran into the kitchen and made popcorn. We are taking care of each other this summer, from Aspen to Cape Cod, Paris to Ireland. Home, that red house with the blue door, is far away, a way station where we do laundry and pack and stay a night. Home. The word, once so solid and steadfast, floats above our heads, just out of our grasp.

And so I teach her to make an omelet. I explain that the

best omelets have three eggs, but since this kitchen in upstate New York has only a tiny frying pan, we will use two. I tell her that two tablespoons of butter are better than one because you can never have enough butter, and that you can fill an omelet with anything you have on hand. Today, garden-fresh tomatoes and crumbs of feta; tomorrow, the American cheese I use to make grilled cheese sandwiches. Omelets make the best of what they are given. I show her how to hold the spatula tenderly so as not to break the egg as it cooks but, rather, to gently lift until it is almost done and then how to sprinkle the filling—the tarragon and Gruyère or basil and fontina—and then the careful folding and finally turning it out of the pan onto the waiting plate.

Annabelle does it all with such care it almost breaks my heart. And then in the crucial final seconds as she folds one side over the other, it tears, and she gasps, "It's ruined! Everything's ruined!" What I know from years of making omelets is that an omelet can always be fixed, even if that means in the end it becomes a plate of delicious scrambled eggs. I take the spatula, say, "Watch," and pat the broken eggs over the tomatoes and cheese. Then I slide it upside down onto the plate—a perfect golden omelet. Annabelle's eyes light up. "It's beautiful," she says. She says, "I will make you an omelet every day."

Before I take my first bite, she touches my hand. "Now make me one?"

I crack two eggs, and begin again.

THE PERFECT OMELET

If there's one thing everyone should know how to make, it's an omelet. The dish is versatile, good for breakfast, lunch, or dinner. It can be served alongside a green salad dressed with a mustardy vinaigrette or in the style preferred by my old favorite Greenwich Village restaurant—with French fries. Omelets are a great way to use up leftovers because anything can go in one. Brickway, a restaurant in Providence, even has a chili omelet. I like mine simpler, with diced ham and cheese. And I am a sucker for what I call a diner omelet, like the one they make at my corner diner, Bus Stop, in New York City (at the corner of Bethune and Hudson, if you're in the neighborhood), which is filled with diced ham and American cheese. This recipe is for the most basic omelet. The rest is up to you and your imagination.

Makes 1 serving

INGREDIENTS

   2 or 3 eggs; I like extra-large
   Pinch of salt
   1 tablespoon unsalted butter
   A handful of diced ham
   *2 slices of American cheese or a handful of fancy cheese like
      Gruyère or aged cheddar, shredded*

1. In a small bowl, beat the eggs and salt with a fork until they're yellow and frothy.

2. Melt the butter over medium heat in a nonstick 10-inch pan (too big a pan will result in scrambled eggs, too small a pan in a mess) until bubbly.

3. Pour in the eggs so that they spread out all over the pan.

4. With a rubber spatula, keep lifting one edge of the eggs and allowing the still liquidy part to flow underneath, until all of the eggs have set.

5. Run a spatula around the edges to loosen.

6. Add ham and cheese on one half of the eggs only, then quickly fold the other half on top of it with that spatula.

7. Have your plate ready and tip the now-folded omelet onto it so that the bottom that was sitting in the pan is now the top of your omelet.

8. You have just made a perfect omelet!

IKEA Life

I am in IKEA starting my life over. In my hands: a pad
and one of those little pencils that brings to mind miniature golf. In front of me: lamps, bedding, desks, rugs, dining room tables, beanbag chairs, media centers, cabinets,
towels, candles, all of it with vaguely Scandinavian names.
The bookcases are Hemnes, Kallax, Tomnas, and they are
built so that you can reconfigure them—stack them tall or
long, symmetrical or not, wide or narrow. I clutch my tiny
pencil, dizzy, queasy, confused. In my old life, the one I had
for almost twenty-five years, the one I had until last week,
my bookshelves were built-in and covered three walls of a
room painted a soothing Bashful Blue. On a beautiful June
day all those years ago, with sunlight streaming through
the paned windows, I'd stood on a ladder and lined up my
books alphabetically on those shelves. Alice Adams to Her-

man Wouk. Now I need to decide between types of shelving with names I can't remember, and long serial numbers, and too many options for how to set them up just to hold my books.

I think of my new empty home waiting for these shelves, and my books, and me. Soaring ceilings, cement floors, big industrial silver pipes, and windows so big that the shades open and close with pulleys. Hemnes, Kallax, Tomnas. Black, white, gray. Across from the shelves are fake living rooms, set up to showcase how the IKEA merchandise can look in your own home. One living room is all red and gray, with modern low furniture. Another is moss green and beige, with inviting throws and pictures of ferns. Another a blue that reminds me of my own lost Bashful Blue, and it is this one that I go to, leaving my pad and pencil on a table I pass, dropping onto the sectional sofa (Soderhamn) and resting my weary head on the striped pillow (Strandkål).

I close my eyes. As I've been told it happens at the end of life, my old life passes in front of me. There I am in Greenwich Village black—jeans, T-shirt, leather biker jacket. There I am marrying the first wrong guy at a big wedding under a tent in a park whose name I've long forgotten. There I am falling in love with another wrong guy, who wears Bermuda red shorts and belts with whales on them. I know— what was I thinking? But we cooked artichokes together and drank a big Tuscan red wine. Once we went to a small candlelit corner restaurant for squid ink pasta. He brought me armfuls of tulips. There I am marrying him on an unusually warm February day, me in a black velvet dress and him in a Nicole Miller tie festooned with champagne bottles and dancing girls. There I am with a baby and then another baby and then a family: slicing cucumbers and peeling apples and tying shoes and packing backpacks and sitting through swimming lessons and ballet lessons and reading Roald Dahl novels and getting covered with sticky kisses.

Oh, this movie of my life.

Even as I lie there on the Bashful Blue Söderhamn sofa I recall Delmore Schwartz's story "In Dreams Begin Responsibilities." He wrote that story during one weekend in July 1935. The title comes from the epigraph for *Responsibilities*, a volume of poetry by Yeats. In the story, a young man dreams he is in a movie theater and realizes the film he's watching is actually documenting his parents' courtship. Eventually, he gets upset and begins to yell at the screen to try to stop them from getting married. "Don't do it! It's not too late to change your minds, both of you. Nothing good will come of it." Several times he breaks down, and he is finally dragged out of the theater by an usher. At the end of the story, the man wakes up and realizes it is the snowy morning of his twenty-first birthday.

Would I stop the film of my own courtship and second marriage if I could? I wonder, my head still down, shoppers bustling around me with their tiny pencils and notepads, designing their lives.

There was the courtship: fast, intense, dizzying.

And there was the marriage: slow, silent, bewildering.

Before him, there was the other marriage in the park. Looking back, I see how brief it was. Five years. A moment, really. I wouldn't undo it. Or perhaps after the span of so many decades, it doesn't matter if it was done or undone. We could never agree on where to live and bounced around, more or less dissatisfied, from apartment to rented house, from city to country. When we finally landed back in Manhattan, where I'd wanted to be all along, we split up. There were tears and sadness, but mostly I remember sitting at the dining room table and dividing up our wedding presents. He took what his side gave us, I took what mine gave. Afterward, I felt relieved.

Before *him,* there was my great love, a man I met on a flight from San Francisco to JFK when I was a flight attendant. He was moving to New York City that very day, all of his belongings in the belly of the plane. We watched the sunset from his window at 47F, dramatic pinks and reds. "You probably are used to seeing this," he said. "I'm not," I told him, leaning across the empty middle seat to see better.

We ran out of short ribs on that flight, and when I told the passenger a few rows ahead of 47F that we had only lasagna left, he began to scream and pound the unit that had the SEAT BELT and NO SMOKING signs on it. He pounded so hard that the overhead compartment popped open and someone's coat fell out. "You gave all of the short ribs to your friends!" he yelled. "You're hiding them!" The pilot was notified, and two male flight attendants restrained the man with special restraints we kept up front for just this kind of problem. I was told to stay in the back of the plane, away from him. When we landed, I had to go to the front door and meet the authorities to issue a report. But then I wouldn't get to talk to 47F again. So I scribbled a note on a cocktail napkin: Dear 47F, If you want someone to show you around the city, this is my phone number. Your flight attendant, Ann. I managed to hand it to him as he left the plane, his face brightening with surprise. "For me?" he asked. That night my phone rang. "This is 47F," he said.

I would not stop this film, I thought from my perch in IKEA. Except I had, after Josh and I spent five years together, and then again after my first marriage ended and we briefly reunited. During that second break, I met the man who would become my second husband. What followed was a brief, confusing time. The chains of old love and the thrill of new love. My boyfriend moved to San Francisco to rediscover himself. The man who I would marry said, "I dreamed we had a son." He said, "Come back to Rhode Island with me." He said, "I love you more than I've ever loved anyone."

My friend Susie auditioned for a famous acting conservatory and got accepted but chose not to go. "I should have gone," she always says, shaking her head with sadness and regret.

My friend Rosemary refused to take a job writing obituaries at a small-town newspaper. "If I had only taken that job," she says, "I would have become a journalist."

If I had not gone to give that talk where he followed me all night, smiling and confident. If I had gone to San Francisco with 47F. If I had said no.

A FAMILY, all worried faces and concern, is staring at me, the woman on the sofa in the fake living room in IKEA.

"I felt weak," I tell them.

But really, I am here starting a new life because I was strong, not weak. Weak was staying and pretending. Weak was crying myself to sleep at night. Weak was pacing the two-hundred-year-old wooden floors at three in the morning, trying to decide.

The family—husband, wife, two wide-eyed children— wait until I stand up before they walk away. I walk away, too. Out of the fake living room, past the bookshelves and lamps. IKEA is a labyrinth—I find myself traveling in circles, passing the shelves again, the Bashful Blue living room. Once I walked a prayer labyrinth in the cathedral at Chartres, France, with the man who was my second husband. I had one baby asleep in a Snugli on my chest, the other clutching my hand. Beautifully preserved, that thirteenth-century, forty-two-foot-wide labyrinth fills the cathedral's nave with its eleven concentric circles and six-lobed rosette at the center. Although no one has been able to document some of the mysteries of the labyrinth—was there once a minotaur in the center? was it a tomb? or a memorial?—what is known is that it symbolized the long, torturous path the pilgrims followed to arrive there.

FOR SIX MONTHS I stayed dizzy, drunk and stupid on love. I gave up my apartment in Greenwich Village and took my cats and myself to Providence. I believed everything. Everything. I would never have to teach or do anything except write. I would go to banquets and balls. He had never loved anyone so much.

THE YEAR MY husband left for a sailing trip in the Caribbean and missed our son's opening night of *Oliver!*, where he sang and danced, an orphan and a pickpocket, and our daughter's debut ballet performance as a snowflake in a white tutu? The call in the middle of the night and his hushed words: *I can't talk, she's here?* The hours he was late, hours and hours. His phone died. He'd misunderstood. He had meetings. All the eye rolling, the silent judgments, the words unsaid, the tears? Mine. His. "You will be sorry if you do not do what you should do," the usher tells the narrator in the Delmore Schwartz story. Is this what held me there? What I should do was stay, pretend I didn't see what I saw, pretend I didn't know what I knew?

I developed insomnia. High blood pressure. Psoriasis.

But how I loved the *idea* of it: a family. Christmas stockings hanging from a mantel, our names stitched on them crookedly by me. Family trips to national parks and national monuments, to the homes of presidents.

Even as I yell at the screen showing my life story, the children make me laugh with their silly songs and misshapen clay George Washingtons. There is the ocean: a birthday dinner on a beach in Mexico, the path lit by candles, the sound of waves, plates of chicken mole and rice and beans. Mojitos on the old city wall in Cartagena. Sailing under the Newport Bridge. Watching for the northern lights on a ship three hundred miles from the Arctic Circle, wrapped in fleece and wool, gazing upward. "It is not right, you will find that out soon enough," the usher says before he drags the narrator from the theater. When does the usher drag *me* out of the theater?

UNLIKE A MAZE, which can dead-end, a labyrinth leads to the center and then back out again. IKEA is all winding aisles that seem to loop back on themselves. I pass lighting again and again. Model kitchens. But how do I exit? I can't quite read the map, which I think tells me I am at the exit, but all I see are those kitchens, those lights. Of course, no one drags you out of the theater. You drag yourself. Even if it takes years, you drag yourself. I know this now. But when you are in it, when you are living it, you forget there is possibility. You forget that you can stop the film at any time and step outside into the "morning already begun."

FINALLY THIS IKEA labyrinth brings me to the escalators and then down to the doors through which I had entered. As I move toward the exit, I smell something familiar. It smells like my childhood home, dinnertime, snowy winter, 1968. It smells like Swedish meatballs. I follow the scent to the IKEA cafeteria, where, past plastic tables and chairs, on a cafeteria food line, I find Swedish meatballs nestled in gravy. IKEA sells 150 million Swedish meatballs a year, the brainchild of its founder, Ingvar Kamprad, who worried that his shoppers would get hungry browsing the aisles of such a massive store. He wanted something cheap and really, really Swedish to serve. Thus, the cafeteria offers salmon and roast beef and reindeer, too.

But it was those Swedish meatballs that kept me from leaving. Not that they tasted extraordinary; they didn't. What they did, on this day when I was starting my new life, was remind me of my oldest home, the one where I grew up. Most nights we ate Italian food, cooked by my Neapolitan grandmother, Mama Rose. Then, on that snowy winter in 1968,

I came home from school to a house filled with the exotic smells of allspice and nutmeg. In the frying pan, tiny meatballs sizzled. I was used to big, meaty meatballs, with garlic and parsley. These were neither big nor garlicky. In another pan, gravy simmered.

"What is this?" I asked Mama Rose.

"Swedish meatballs," she said. "From the Galloping Gourmet."

It was no secret that Mama Rose had a crush on Graham Kerr, the Galloping Gourmet. She watched him every afternoon, spellbound. But never had she re-created one of his unfamiliar, often French (Mama Rose would never have anything to do with anything or anyone French) recipes.

"Swedish," she repeated, as if she had read my mind.

A few hours later, the Swedish meatballs appeared atop a tangle of egg noodles. I tasted one, and swooned. The spices, the combination of pork and beef, the gravy—all of it combined into a taste sensation like I'd never known. I felt sophisticated, adult, worldly. *Swedish meatballs.*

Now here I was, forty years later, coming in a strange way, full circle. Another labyrinth, perhaps. Another film of my life. I had no bookshelves or lighting. My old home was empty, except for the boxes packed and waiting for the Gentle Giants to take them away. My new home waited, too—to be filled. Tomorrow, I decided, I would return to IKEA with a plan: two floor lamps (Holmö), four bookcases (Hemnes, white), a bed for my daughter (Brimnes, white). Just when I'd

felt lost and confused—new home, new beginning—I'd been
returned to a long-ago snowy night when I'd discovered,
through a small, strange meatball, the world of possibility.

GOGO'S SWEDISH MEATBALLS
WITH IKEA GRAVY

I swear to you that I ask Gogo to make me her Swedish meatballs *almost* as much as I ask her to make me her regular meatballs. The two kinds of meatballs could not be more different.
Unlike the ones we eat with spaghetti and red sauce, the
Swedish ones have allspice and pork and they are bite-sized
morsels covered in brown gravy and served over egg noodles. But here's the thing: Gogo uses bottled brown gravy.
IKEA makes its own gravy, and the recipe is easy to find
online, so I'm sharing it here with you. Please don't tell Gogo,
who, despite being a fabulous cook, likes to use things like
cream of mushroom soup and frozen veggies and . . . well . . .
bottled gravy.

Serves 6 to 8

For the meatballs:

INGREDIENTS

   2 pounds ground beef, 86 percent lean
   1 pound ground pork

1 onion, chopped fine

2 eggs

2 teaspoons allspice

2 teaspoons salt

½ teaspoon pepper

Canola oil

1. Mix all the ingredients, except the oil, together well.
2. Roll into small balls.
3. Fry in the hot oil in batches until browned.
4. Drain.
5. Simmer in the gravy as directed below.

For the IKEA gravy:

INGREDIENTS

2 tablespoons unsalted butter

2 tablespoons flour

1½ cups beef broth

1 teaspoon Worcestershire sauce

¼ cup heavy cream

Salt and pepper to taste

2 tablespoons chopped flat-leaf parsley

1. Melt the butter in a skillet over medium heat.
2. Add the flour and whisk until smooth.
3. Add beef broth and Worcestershire sauce and keep whisking until the mixture reaches a simmer.

4. Add the heavy cream and the cooked meatballs.
5. Reduce the heat to medium low and simmer until the gravy thickens, about 10 minutes.
6. Season with salt and pepper to taste.
7. Sprinkle with the parsley.

How to Cook Fish When You Really, Really Do Not Like Fish

I was with a man for over twenty-five years who did not love to eat or to cook. How I could stay so long with someone who didn't enjoy two of the things I enjoy most is bewildering to me, but it does—in part—explain why he is now my ex-husband. On one of our first dates, we did cook together. We steamed artichokes. We made Bolognese. We ate it all up, the artichokes with a homemade vinaigrette and the Bolognese with fresh pasta from Raffetto's on West Houston Street, and a loaf from Amy's Bread warmed in the oven and dipped into grassy olive oil. I lived then in a duplex on Leroy Street in Greenwich Village, with a galley kitchen and a dining room table that had been gouged with a knife during a robbery. As we sat at that table with the deep curving scar cut into it, eating the dinner we'd shopped for and cooked together, I could imagine a lifetime of meals like this with this man, someone I hardly knew but had swept into my life like a tornado, turning everything upside down. Had I known then that this would be the first and last meal we shopped for and cooked together, would I have hidden in the basement instead of opening my arms and letting the tornado carry me away? I cannot say, of course. But I can say that the memory of that meal was enough for a while, until it wasn't anymore.

This man had grown up in a large family with a mother who was not a very good or interested cook. Food was fuel. It kept you warm in winter, helped you grow, and gave you the things you needed to be healthy. One of his complaints when we had dinner parties was that the food wasn't simple enough. Simple? I wanted to spend all day Saturday in the kitchen, a recipe propped up before me, dicing and sautéing and grinding spices. A homemade mole with four kinds of peppers and toasted bread and Mexican chocolate. A make-your-own taco party with six different fillings and rice and beans. Wild mushroom lasagna. Jambalaya. A twelve-hour pork butt in Cuban spices. Planning and cooking and serving food to friends made me happy. Not him, though. He didn't understand that joy, just as I didn't understand why someone would ride a bike across the state for fun or climb Mount Washington in November.

Mostly I pored over my cookbooks and made a week's plan for dinners. He ate whatever I made, sometimes getting up to rinse off the sauce, sometimes saying the dinner was good. What is this? he'd ask, and I'd tell him I'd made it dozens of times before. If I asked him what he wanted for dinner, he always said the same thing: How about salmon?

I have had salmon that I liked very much. Copper River

salmon, in June, in Oregon, to be exact. The meat is red and the fish is fresh and it is available for only a minute, or so it seems. But mostly, I don't like salmon. In fact, I kind of hate it. The insipid color. The pin bones. The fatty texture. The taste. Yet if every night of the week you make anything you desire and for just one night your husband wants salmon, it seems a fair thing to do to make that salmon.

Someone gave me a recipe for salmon that I used a lot. Put the salmon in a glass baking dish. Grate lots of ginger over it and cover it with bottled teriyaki sauce. Let it sit for an hour, then grill it. The teriyaki covered up the taste of the salmon, anyway. But except for the ginger, it wasn't exactly the freshest way to prepare it.

After a while, I stopped making salmon. Then he asked for swordfish, my second-least-favorite fish. Usually swordfish is served cut thick as steaks, the flesh a weird grayish color, and fishy-tasting. My father used to slather swordfish steaks with mayo and stick them on the grill, which did make them moist, at least. I tried that. And kebabs. And a fancy marinade from Whole Foods. Like with the salmon, it all just served to mask the taste of the fish, for which I was happy. But basically it was like drinking teriyaki or fancy marinade, with a kick of fish at the end.

I admit that it's unusual to have grown up in and to live again as an adult in the state known as the Ocean State and not like fish. Maybe this comes from all of my childhood Christmas Eves, when, like all good Neapolitans, we celebrated *La Vigilia,* or the Feast of the Seven Fishes. Our seven

fishes were eel, snails, *baccalà*, anchovies, smelts, shrimp, and squid. Imagine being six or eight years old and staring at a plate of eel and snails. I used to cry at the smell and the sight of those seven fishes. I used to cry watching my aunts and uncles drop fried smelts into their mouths whole and slather anchovies on their spaghetti. If I didn't eat the seven fishes, I got that spaghetti with no butter or oil or cheese, a pile of tepid, gluey pasta.

Or maybe I just don't like fish. Give me a sautéed soft-shell crab, lobster dipped in butter, *moules frites*, or stuffed quahogs, and I'm happy. But fish, unless it's very fresh and deep-fried and served with homemade tartar sauce and a pile of real French fries? No thank you.

Of course, it wasn't just my then husband who craved salmon or swordfish. There were vegetarians who came for dinner. Pescatarians. People on diets. Sometimes pork butt, even one cooked for twelve hours in sour orange and garlic, was not acceptable. So I made it a personal mission to find ways to cook fish that even I would like. It didn't save my marriage, but it did save a few dinner parties.

COUSIN CHIPPY'S
SWORDFISH OREGANATO

Cousin Chippy makes a great Sunday supper: all kinds of meats (pork ribs, flank steak, sausage, etc.) cooked in red

sauce and served with pasta. He grills pizza on his Parthenon-shaped pizza oven in Breezy Point, New York, and cooks big country ribs in it all night, in the dying embers. And he made me one of the few fish dishes I actually liked. I asked him for the recipe, and he wrote it in pencil on a ripped piece of cardboard. This preparation is a popular Sicilian dish, sometimes called swordfish with salmoriglio sauce. *Salmoriglio* derives from a word that means "brine," and the swordfish does sit in a salty, lemony mixture. That part is easy. The tricky part is making sure the swordfish steaks are cut ¼ to ½ inch thick, the thinner the better. My fishmonger always growls at me when I ask him to cut the fish thin, but it makes all the difference, and even fish haters like me enjoy the results.

Serves 4

INGREDIENTS

> *Four 8-ounce swordfish steaks cut ¼ to ½ inch thick*
> *1 cup olive oil*
> *Juice of 3 or 4 lemons*
> *¼ cup chopped fresh oregano*
> *A handful of kosher salt*
> *Arugula*
> *Lemon slices*

1. Combine the olive oil, lemon juice, oregano, and salt.
2. Immerse the swordfish in the marinade and leave in the fridge for 30 to 60 minutes.
3. Prepare your grill (or indoor grill pan) for high heat.

4. Let the excess marinade drip off the swordfish and place the steaks on the grill. They will cook up fast—just a minute or less per side—so keep an eye on them.

5. Serve on top of arugula with lemon slices on top of the swordfish. If you're feeling fancy, grill the lemon slices, too.

GREEN HERB SAUCE

From *The San Francisco Chronicle Cookbook,*
Volume II, edited by Michael Bauer and Fran Irwin

I have my father, Rod McKuen, and my old boyfriend Josh to thank for my love of San Francisco. Let me explain. When my father was first in the navy, in the late 1940s, he was stationed in San Francisco, a city he loved. (One of my greatest pleasures was taking him back there when I was a TWA flight attendant.) He used to describe the Victorian houses in Pacific Heights, Lombard Street—the crookedest street in the world!—and the fog and the food and the allure of that beautiful city, where he was engaged for a time to a Nob Hill heiress. By the time I started reading Rod McKuen's poetry about Stanyan Street and fog and rain and love, I had determined that someday I would live there, too, and unravel its mysteries. That never came to pass. But for many happy years, I was in love with a guy from San Francisco, and he shared with me all of its pleasures, culinary and cultural. It's no surprise, then, that when I found *The San Francisco Chronicle Cookbook*, I bought it and made many of its recipes. This green herb sauce, from the second volume, is by Marion Cunningham and works perfectly on salmon—both hiding that salmony taste I dislike and highlighting the fresh herbs. With light greens and this sauce, you can make a salmon salad that even I enjoy.

INGREDIENTS

5 garlic cloves, chopped
Juice and grated zest of 2 lemons
1 cup chopped cilantro
1 cup chopped basil
½ cup chopped Italian parsley
1 cup olive oil
1 teaspoon salt
½ teaspoon freshly ground pepper

1. Combine first five ingredients in a bowl.
2. Stir in the olive oil, salt, and pepper.
3. Taste and add more salt if needed.

NOTE: I have been known to use more or less of each herb as my pantry dictated, and to throw the herbs unchopped into the food processor with the garlic, then add the olive oil and salt and pepper. You really can't ruin this sauce.

Three Potato

In 1988, I was invited to teach at the esteemed Bread Loaf Writers' Conference in Vermont for the first time. A few years earlier, I had attended as a student, clutching my three connected short stories nervously, unsure of what exactly was supposed to happen at such a place. I didn't know that Robert Frost had started it in 1926, or that some of my favorite writers—Eudora Welty, Willa Cather, Anne Sexton—had been there. I only knew that my teacher William Decker, in one of the only creative writing classes I ever took, told me that I was "the real thing, a real writer," and that real writers went to Bread Loaf. So I went. There, workshop leader Nicholas Delbanco urged me to turn those short stories into a novel, and always the good student, I went home and did just that. *Somewhere off the Coast of Maine* was published in 1987, and I won a fellowship to return to Bread Loaf and work with Hilma Wolitzer. A year later, I found myself back on the mountain as a faculty member, teamed up with Tim O'Brien.

I remember a lot about those long-ago two weeks in Vermont. I remember lying on my back in a field full of writers, watching shooting stars. I remember feeling a strange mixture of shyness and gregariousness in the faculty lounge in Treman, where we drank Bloody Marys before lunch and gin and tonics before dinner. I remember sneaking into Middlebury for dinner with William Matthews and other writers, drinking wine I couldn't afford.

What I don't remember is walking arm in arm with two friends out of the inn and a man calling out to me: "Miss Hood?" I don't remember turning and smiling at that man, who was a twenty-five-year-old writer there as a scholar for an article he'd written about his mentor, Reynolds Price. I've been told—by him—that I asked him what it was he wanted to do, but I don't remember that. Nor do I remember that he told me he wanted to write fiction and I told him, "You will!" and then I walked away.

Twenty years later, I was teaching at a writers' conference in Cleveland, Ohio, happily sitting with a Cleveland friend, waiting for the afternoon lecture, when a very cute guy walked in. That cute guy was the same guy I'd walked away from that long-ago summer at Bread Loaf, although I didn't know that until he stood at the podium and said, "Ann Hood doesn't know this, but I've been in love with her for twenty years." A statement like that gets my attention. Of course he meant the literary-crush kind of love, but for a writer that's even better than the other kind of love.

Even more years had to pass before it turned into love love, years with intermittent e-mails, exchanging our books, a brief drink at the Miami Book Fair, and ultimately marriages that had gone bad. One night we looked at each other and, as corny as it sounds, we both knew. It was kind of like, *Oh! It's you!*

When I was a teenager, I used to cry to my mother, "Will anyone ever love me? I mean really love me? For me?" And she would always say that there was someone who would love me truly for who I was. "How will I know it's love?" I'd ask her. "You just know," she always said. After two marriages, I questioned my judgment on this "just knowing" business. But for some of us, like me, finding that person takes a lot longer, and you need to make some mistakes along the way.

What I know for sure is that this man is perfect *for me*. He loves to read and talk about literature. He loves to play cards. He is a writer, and he works hard as a writer. He loves to travel. He even learned to knit. And he is a cook. For a long time, if I said I liked a particular food—chicken fried steak, for example—he'd say: "I have to cook that for you!" And if I said I didn't like something—baked potatoes, for example—he'd say, "You'll like mine." And he was right.

And so I offer you the recipe for Michael's Baked Potatoes, because he made me fall in love with baked potatoes, and with him.

MICHAEL'S BAKED POTATOES

When I asked Michael for his baked potato recipe for this book, he thought it was one of the funniest recipe requests he'd ever heard. And he told me the story about a babysitter he'd had when he was around four. He kept telling her there wasn't enough butter on his potato, so this old woman sat there and rubbed an entire stick of butter on his halved baked potato. She was baffled when he said, "There's still not enough butter." To which I asked, "Is there ever enough butter?" Michael says that a good baked potato is all about texture. I have to agree—that's why I never liked those wrinkled ones of my childhood. Basically, according to Michael, you are basically making mashed potatoes in a shell. Preferably a very hard shell.

Serves 4

INGREDIENTS

4 medium-sized russet potatoes, well washed
1 stick butter, divided into quarters (plus more for the table),
    warmed to room temperature
Kosher salt, to taste

1. Preheat the oven to 425 degrees F.
2. Put the potatoes in it.
3. After an hour, squeeze one. If it's soft, continue to bake

for 15 more minutes, or until the shell is distinctly hard and the inner potato is completely soft.

4. Remove from the oven and immediately cut a slit down the middle lengthwise, to allow the steam out (otherwise, it might soften the shell).

5. Pinch the slit from each end to open it wider and gently separate the flesh from the shell, chopping it to break it up (without removing it from the shell) with a fork.

6. Add half of one of the butter quarters and chop it into the potato.

7. Add the other half and continue to chop until the butter is evenly distributed.

8. Repeat with the other potatoes and butter quarters.

9. Serve immediately.

Make sure there's more room-temperature butter and salt on the table so people can add more to the potato's flesh or to the shell after the inside has been devoured.

NOTE: If making this dish for a larger group, remove the flesh from all the potatoes and mash it together with butter and salt, then distribute among the shells (which you can crisp in the oven). You can also add minced onion or other fun stuff to the flesh before distributing it, top each potato with grated cheddar cheese, and bake until the cheese melts.

With Thanks to the Chicken

M y father used to stick an apple in a chicken's butt before he roasted it. If he was out of apples, he used a peeled orange. "Keeps it moist," he said.

I don't know if he was right, but his roast chicken was indeed moist, and he made a delicious homemade gravy using the pan drippings, flour, and milk. With mashed potatoes, I can't think of a more satisfying Sunday supper.

When my kids were young, I often roasted a chicken for supper, because it is the easiest thing to make. Sometimes I would sit the chicken in the roasting pan on top of baby carrots and fingerling potatoes, so that our entire meal cooked in that one pan, the veggies browned in chicken fat, the chicken moist not from apples but from the halved lemon I put in its cavity. I put in a halved head of garlic, too, and whatever fresh herb I had handy—rosemary or thyme or tarragon.

What my father didn't do was use that carcass for stock the way I do with my turkey carcass at Thanksgiving.

I have hosted Thanksgiving since my son, Sam, was born—in other words, for twenty-five years. That first time, seven-month-old Sam and I lived on the top floor of a restored Colonial, his father having flown the coop, so to speak. We had two bedrooms, maybe three if you counted the odd alcove off my bedroom, and an eat-in kitchen, where my cousin Gloria-Jean and I somehow managed to fit a dozen people. We even made them do crafts: tracing their hands onto construction paper and fashioning turkeys from them with dime-store feathers glued to the fingers. My father famously even drew in his watch, which sat jauntily below the turkey's neck. That night, after everyone left, I put the turkey carcass into a big pot of water and simmered it all the next day, a practice I continued for every Thanksgiving night afterward. The dinner the evening after Thanksgiving was always turkey pot pie made with leftover turkey, gravy, and whatever vegetables remained—some years green beans and carrots, others peas and potatoes. And the second evening after Thanksgiving I simmered that stock and cooked either rice or egg noodles in it for a final farewell to the holiday, and to the turkey, which in between had been put into cold sandwiches with mayo and cranberry sauce and hot open-faced sandwiches topped with gravy.

My family has enjoyed over two decades of hosting Thanksgiving and the rituals of it—yes, the cooking with cousins and friends, but also the various people (opera singers from the Czech Republic, exchange students from Germany and Japan and Brazil, West Point cadets) around the table with us, trying to remember how to set the timer on the oven (*where* did I put the instructions for the stove?) so that one turkey would start to roast at six a.m., the party the night before that often led to conga lines and washing kale in the bathtub and someone crying in the bathroom, the arranging of tables across three rooms to accommodate eighteen or twenty-two or thirty-one people, the taking down of the mismatched champagne glasses and wineglasses, the toasts and the going around the tables to say what we are thankful for, watching as the little kids grow out of the kids' table and become teenagers deserving a room of their own to eat in, right off the dining room, and seeing the teenagers grow up and away.

There was the year the Romanian exchange student turned the oven off when the timer started. The year the kitchen caught on fire the Monday before Thanksgiving and we had to buy a new stove and get it delivered before Wednesday. The year Sam and his cousin painted the wall of our rented house; the year Annabelle and her friends emptied all of the clothes out of the closets. The year after Grace died, when I ran into the street screaming and pulling my hair, grief so enormous and consuming that I could not take all that food and all those people.

But always, always, the turkey stock the next day. The turkey pot pie. The soup. The sandwiches, hot and cold.

One year I had no rice or egg noodles, so I boiled tortellini in the stock and a new tradition was born: Tortellini en Brodo.

But I wanted to talk about chicken.

Two years ago, Annabelle and I left that house that had hosted so many Thanksgivings and moved into a loft in a renovated factory (where we had just as grand a Thanksgiving as we'd ever had, with just as many friends and family). Before I had unpacked all of our boxes, I made a simple dinner for us of a rotisserie chicken from the grocery store and green beans. Cleaning up, I looked at that carcass and had one thought: soup. Why it took me over two decades to realize that my chicken dinner could give me exactly what my Thanksgiving turkey had, I cannot say. But that night I found my orange Le Creuset Dutch oven, and the next morning I covered the carcass with water and simmered it all day. The aroma made my new place smell like home. That night, Annabelle and I feasted on Tortellini en Brodo in rich chicken stock.

My husband, Michael, who is full of good ideas, told me that there was no reason to wait until the next day to get that stock simmering—I could do it overnight by placing the carcass, covered in water, in a pot in a 180 degree oven. I added carrots, didn't I? he asked me. And onion? I didn't, but I do now.

Time passes and everything changes. Or not everything, I suppose, but most things. New rituals are born, even as we hold on to or adapt the old ones. One night a week, Annabelle and I have a chicken dinner. While we sleep, stock is made in the oven. The next night we slurp Tortellini en Brodo, leaving enough for her to have a bowl of it for breakfast and a thermos full for lunch at school the next day. This we will do, I suppose, until she grows up and leaves for college. Until then, I keep lemons on hand to make our chicken moist, and tortellini in the freezer for our soup. It's true: chicken soup cures everything.

MY ROAST CHICKEN

I roast a chicken once a week, and with the stock I make from its bones, we have Tortellini en Brodo for dinner, breakfast, and a thermos full for Annabelle's lunch. These are the simplest, most nourishing meals you can make, and if you cook nothing else at home, please at least roast a chicken, make stock, and have Tortellini en Brodo. You're welcome.

Serves 4 to 8

INGREDIENTS
   One 6-pound chicken
   A bag of baby carrots, 1 chopped onion, fingerling potatoes
      (optional)
   Salt and pepper
   2 lemons, halved (or an apple or orange, halved)
   1 bunch thyme or rosemary or both
   Unpeeled head of garlic cut in half longways
   3 tablespoons unsalted butter, melted

1. Preheat the oven to 425 degrees F.
2. Remove the stuff inside the chicken and dry the chicken with paper towels.
3. If you are using the optional veggies, place them in a roasting pan and plop the chicken on top of them; if not, just plop the chicken in the pan.
4. Salt and pepper the chicken, inside and out.
5. Stick the lemon, herbs, and garlic up its butt.
6. Pour the melted butter over it.
7. Roast for 1½ hours or until the little red thing pops out.

MICHAEL'S OVERNIGHT CHICKEN STOCK

My husband invented this way of making stock, and even though I'm a bit biased, I think it's brilliant. While you sleep, your chicken is making you a rich, delicious stock! What could be easier?

Makes enough stock to cook 1 pound of tortellini

INGREDIENTS

The carcass of your chicken, broken up so that you can easily cover all of it with water
2 leeks, cut in half
2 carrots, cut in half

1. Smash up the chicken carcass and put it in your Dutch oven with the leeks and the carrots.
2. Add enough water to cover everything by an inch.
3. Stick the pot in the oven, covered (otherwise it will boil), and set the oven to 180 degrees F.
4. Go to bed.
5. Wake up and you have chicken stock!

TORTELLINI EN BRODO

This soup takes about 7 minutes to make. Take that chicken stock you made while you were sleeping (or 4 quarts of store-bought stock), bring it to a boil, and add a pound of tortellini. Cook until the tortellini is al dente, about seven minutes. Serve with grated Parmesan. If you want to get fancy, add frozen peas and garnish with chopped flat-leaf parsley. Some people cook the tortellini separately so they will not absorb the chicken stock and swell and soften. Then they add them to the stock after they're cooked. I am not one of those people.

Let Us Now Praise
the English Muffin

My husband, Michael, knows how to cook. He trained at the Culinary Institute of America, and he writes famous cookbooks with famous chefs, and he writes his own cookbooks, too, and wins James Beard awards. (He has also written other things, wonderful nonfiction books and a glorious collection of three novellas. Have I mentioned I'm in love?) But there are two things he cannot change my mind about when it comes to food: the deliciousness of American cheese (oh, please, it is the best cheese for a grilled cheese sandwich, especially on Wonder bread and served with Campbell's tomato soup, made with added milk instead of water and a dusting of celery salt—right now the man I love is cringing as he reads this over my shoulder) and the fact that Thomas' English muffins are the superior—no, the *only*—English muffin. He prefers a different brand, one that is also delicious. But to me, *Thomas'* and *English muffin* are synonymous.

I cannot say that I grew up on English muffins; we were not an English muffin kind of family. We sometimes ate Sunbeam bread, which we called either bond bread or American bread, because what we mostly ate was crusty Italian bread, which we dipped into spaghetti sauce for after-school snacks or stuffed with meatballs and gravy or sausage and peppers or stew (which was beef chuck cut into chunks and simmered with celery, potatoes, and carrots in tomato sauce; the first time I ate the other kind of beef stew I felt confused). Sometimes, at restaurants, when a waitress asks my mother what kind of bread she'd like with her meal, my mother says, "American bread."

But back to English muffins.

In Victorian England, they were eaten by the downstairs servants. The family baker made English muffins from a combination of leftover bread and biscuit dough scraps and mashed potatoes fried on a hot griddle. (The oven as we know it did not yet exist.) But families upstairs were no fools. Once they tasted these muffins, they wanted them for themselves. The word "muffin," by the way, is thought to derive from either the French *moufflet,* the term for a soft bread, or the Low German *muffen,* meaning "little cakes." Before long, English muffin factories appeared, and muffin men, with wooden trays around their necks filled with muffins, walked the streets hawking these little bites of deliciousness, the inspiration for the traditional child's song with the line "Do you know the muffin man?" Famously, in my family, my brother sang that song in his kindergarten play. In fancier homes and clubs, the muffins were split open, toasted, and served at teatime.

Some people confuse English muffins with crumpets, but the difference is clear: crumpets use baking powder to create the characteristic "holes" on their outside to trap butter and other toppings. An English muffin's holes are on the inside. And it was an immigrant from Plymouth, England, named Samuel Bath Thomas who invented the English muffin I love so much. Thomas came to New York City looking for opportunity when he was twenty-one years old, and six years later, in 1880, he opened his own bakery, at 163 Ninth Avenue in Chelsea. There, he perfected the muffins and precut them— what we call "fork-split" today—so people could pull them apart without crushing the soft dough. There were thousands of bakeries in New York City back then, but Thomas's muffins appealed to hoteliers, who thought they were fancier than plain old toast. Soon, Thomas opened a second bakery, at 337 West Twentieth Street, in a building that is still known as "the Muffin Building."

I don't know when I first tasted an English muffin—at a breakfast place somewhere? Or maybe under the Canadian bacon and poached egg and hollandaise of an eggs Benedict? All I know is that I love the combination of soft and crunch, the nooks and crannies, the perfect size—smaller than toast but big enough to hold a sandwich of chopped avocado, bacon, and lettuce. I buy a six-pack of English muffins every week. When my kids were little, I made them a snack of an English muffin, spaghetti sauce, and melted mozzarella: English muffin pizzas. Even now, almost every day at around eleven a.m. I toast an English muffin, and while it's toasting I ponder the endless ways I can eat it. Crunchy peanut butter, sliced banana, drizzled honey. Butter and good strawberry jam. English muffin, breakfast sausage patty, fried egg, melted American (sorry, my beloved!) cheese.

I have had sourdough made from old San Francisco starter and tart rye and bread studded with salty, expensive olives. I have even had arguably the most famous bread in the world, the Poilâne loaf, which is made in Paris from only four ingredients—sourdough, stone-ground wheat flour, water, and sea salt from Guérande—then baked in a wood-burning oven and stamped with a large fancy *P*. And although I sometimes dream of these breads, they do not give me what the English muffin does. I do not have to cross an ocean or a continent for it. Instead, I simply walk into my grocery store, and in no time I am standing in my kitchen beside my toaster, butter knife or jam jar or poached egg in hand, ready for lunch.

ITALIAN BEEF STEW

Here are two ways to use English muffins that I like to make in a pinch. Lightly toast two English muffins. Warm leftover red sauce (see "Gogo's Sauce," page 151) and top each half with it. Add shredded mozzarella and put the muffins in the microwave or under the broiler or in a warmed oven just long enough to melt the cheese. Sprinkle grated Parmesan on top and you've got an English muffin pizza.

For breakfast, lightly toast an English muffin. Cook two breakfast sausage patties according to the package's directions. Poach two eggs by cracking them one by one into a bowl, then adding each into rapidly boiling water. Turn off the heat, cover the pan, and let it sit for four minutes. Remove the eggs with a slotted spoon. Put the cooked sausage on the toasted English muffin. Top each side with a poached egg. Drape a piece of American or Swiss cheese on top, and heat in the oven until the cheese melts. Better than an Egg McMuffin!

However, everybody who has read this essay, besides putting in a vote for their favorite brand of English muffin, wants to know how to make the Italian Beef Stew. So here it is:

Serves 6

INGREDIENTS

3 pounds top round beef, trimmed and cut into 2-inch chunks
Salt and pepper to taste
1 onion, chopped
6 potatoes cut into chunks roughly the size of the meat
4 carrots, chopped
1 celery stalk, chopped
One 28-ounce can tomato sauce
Vegetable oil

1. Coat a Dutch oven with oil and turn the heat to medium high.
2. Generously salt and pepper both sides of the meat.
3. Brown the meat in the oil over medium-high heat.
4. Add the veggies and stir until fork tender but not soft.
5. Add the tomato sauce and enough water to cover the meat and veggies, if necessary. (A tip: Use the empty unwashed can for water. That way you'll get whatever's clinging inside.)
6. Cover and simmer for about one hour, or until the meat is very tender.
7. Let it rest, even overnight, before reheating and serving with crusty Italian bread.

NOTE: This stew is not thick like an Irish beef stew. However, if you want the broth a little thicker, make a slurry by putting a couple of tablespoons of flour or cornstarch into a bowl and mixing in about ½ cup of the hot broth until it combines. (If it's too thick, just add a little more broth.) Then add it to the stew, stirring to thicken.

Comfort Food II

Here is, as E. E. Cummings wrote, the deepest secret nobody knows, the root of the root and the bud of the bud: I am sad. A lot. There are times when I can't catch my breath because I am so sad. Sometimes I wake at three or four in the morning feeling like I am having a heart attack. But I realize soon enough that what is gripping me is not a literal seizing of my heart. It is, instead, a metaphorical one. My broken heart is seizing up again, remembering, aching, sobbing.

What I want to say, to believe, is that it gets better. And in some ways it does. God forgive me, days and days pass in which I don't think about Grace. How this can be so, I don't know. When she first died, not even a second passed without my thinking of her. Or of the *absence* of her. During those first weeks, someone told me that she'd lost a daughter long ago. "But recently," she said, "I was in Borders buying books and I was writing a check and when I filled in the date, I paused. It was the day my daughter had died, years ago." I remember thinking what a relief that would be. I remember thinking how terrible that would be.

I don't think I ever will forget that day. April 18, 2002. In fact, I remember it kinesthetically before my brain remembers it.

This year, in mid-March, I was overwhelmed by the desire to knit. Not just to knit, but to knit something hard. I knit all the time, mostly cotton dishrags in happy colors. Also lots of hats—lately in a soft alpaca I discovered at Yarnia in Nacogdoches, Texas. And fingerless mitts to keep my sweetheart's hands warm. But come March, these projects were not enough. I needed something hard. So I signed up for a tutorial on knitting arm warmers with a technique called helical stripes, which I'd never even heard of before, on four double-pointed needles, which I hadn't knit with since the year Grace died and I developed an obsession with knitting socks on them. I watched a lot of YouTube tutorials: how to cast on with those needles, how to join your knitting in the round, and, of course, how to knit helical stripes. I dropped stitches, one night two-thirds of them, or forty-eight. My knitting had holes and ladders (don't ask). I knit and I unknit, sitting on my sofa and flying in airplanes. My friend Mary, who had also embarked on this helical-stripe journey, gave up in frustration—she who knits sweaters without patterns. But I, lazy dishrag knitter, persisted. I loved how impossible that arm warmer was, how I had to keep focused and reread directions. How I had to keep my head down. How those stripes mostly were perfect, chasing each other around my tiny needles.

"I just need to knit for a while," I told my sweetheart.

"I'll knit a few rows, then start supper," I told my daughter.

Deadlines called to me. Novels waited to be read. *I think I'll just knit,* I said to myself.

I made a thumb gusset. A cuff. I cast off. One arm warmer was finished, albeit imperfectly. This is the point in many a knitter's life when joy turns to disappointment: we must start over again and knit the second one.

But not me. On April 1, a snowstorm hit New England. There was nothing to do except knit. I cast on those seventy-two stitches and with glee began all over again.

It wasn't until a few days later that my mind caught up with the rest of me. April 18 loomed. I was knitting to keep grief at bay, as I'd done that first terrible year and for so many years that followed. But, of course, knitting only softens the sadness. Nothing takes it away.

That sadness doesn't just arrive in April. It still hits me when I see Seckel pears in the grocery store. Little blond girls in glasses. Hear the Beatles singing "Eight Days a Week." The sharp stab of a memory rises to the surface out of nowhere.

Oh, Grace!

Like knitting, there is food that offers comfort. Emily Post wrote in 1922 that we should feed the grief-stricken simple broth. Me, I make a doctored ramen. I poach an egg in it and add butter and American cheese. I put it in a big orange bowl and eat it, every drop.

When, this April, I put my knitting down long enough to get up to make that soup that comforts me and found I was, foolishly, out of ramen, I turned to my second-best comfort food: grilled cheese. (Perhaps the key to soothing my aching heart is American cheese?) My usual simple version—white bread buttered on the outside with that cheese in the middle—didn't feel like enough for how much comfort I needed that day. So I tried a recipe of Ruth Reichl's that included mayonnaise and cheese on the outside and butter and cheese on the inside. Yes. That did the trick. I ate that crunchy, gooey sandwich, the plate in my lap as I sat on the sofa. When I finished, I picked up those double-pointed needles, and I carefully knit helical stripes. Outside, the sky was silvery gray. Sometimes, even in April, it feels like spring will never come.

Riffs on Comfort Food

You have probably noticed that this essay is called "Comfort Food II," which raises a question: Where is "Comfort Food I"? The answer is that it is an essay I wrote not long after Grace died; it appeared in the literary journal *Alimentum,* as well as in my memoir *Comfort: A Journey Through Grief.* That essay talks about taking comfort in eating Grace's favorite dinner: sliced cucumbers and pasta with butter and Parmesan. I eat this meal every year on September 24, her birthday.

I would love it if you did, too, and thought about Grace as you ate.

Knitting and this soup or a grilled cheese sandwich will help take the blues away. I promise. If you don't knit, then read a good crime novel, preferably by Laura Lippman or Denise Mina or Tana French. Stay under a quilt. Mend.

PERFECT INSTANT RAMEN

By chef Roy Choi, who shared it with the *New York Times* in 2014 and said, "It's our snack, it's our peanut butter and jelly sandwich, it's our bowl of cereal. It's something that's been part of my life forever."

Makes 1 serving

INGREDIENTS

1 pack ramen noodles, chicken flavor
1 large egg
½ teaspoon butter
2 slices American cheese

NOTE: Roy Choi's recipe calls for ¼ teaspoon toasted sesame seeds and the green part of half a scallion, thinly sliced. I have made this with sesame seeds and scallions, but mostly I don't have them on hand when the blues hit, and the soup is delicious without them.

1. Bring 2½ cups water to a boil.
2. Add the ramen noodles and cook for 2 minutes.
3. Stir in the flavor packet.
4. Remove the pan from the heat and gently add the egg to it. *Do not stir!* Just kind of pull the noodles over the egg and let it sit for a minute.
5. Carefully pour into a bowl and add the butter and the cheese, torn into pieces, and then the sesame seeds and the scallion, if you're using them.

PERFECT GRILLED CHEESE

I think it's important to state that I am happy with the most basic grilled cheese sandwich: I butter four slices of white bread, melt a lot of butter in a skillet, put two slices of the bread buttered side down in the pan, top those slices with a couple pieces of American cheese, then top that with the two other slices of bread, buttered side up, flip it, and as soon as it's browned and the cheese is melted, I have two pretty perfect sandwiches. However, Ruth Reichl takes grilled cheese to another level by using mayo. Yes. Mayo. Apparently chef Gabrielle Hamilton, owner of one of my favorite New York City restaurants, Prune, also uses mayo. These women know what they're talking about, obviously. The sandwich here is "adapted" from Reichl's recipe from her must-have cookbook, *My Kitchen Year*. I say adapted because her recipe calls for garlic and any combination of shallots, leeks, scallions, and onions, and I leave those out. I never have onion on my hamburger, either. I'm not an onion-in-my-sandwich kind of person.

Makes 1 sandwich

INGREDIENTS

A couple big handfuls of shredded cheddar
Unsalted butter
2 slices of sturdy white bread
Mayonnaise

1. Butter one side of a slice of bread and heap some shredded cheese on it, buttered side facing in. Top with another slice, also with the buttered side in.
2. Spread a thin layer of mayo on the outside of both slices.
3. Press more grated cheese into the mayo.
4. Fry in melted butter in a skillet until browned and oozy.

Tomato Pie

It is that time in summer when the basil starts taking over my yard and local tomatoes are finally ripe, red, and misshapen and so juicy that when I cut into one, I need to wipe down the counter. In other words, it's the perfect confluence of ingredients for tomato pie. And not just any tomato pie, but Laurie Colwin's Tomato Pie, a feast of tomatoes and cheese and basil baked into a double biscuit crust.

I first discovered this recipe before I was married, in a long-ago *Gourmet* magazine. I ripped it out and took it with me for a week with my parents and assorted relatives in a rented house at Scarborough Beach in Narragansett, Rhode Island. There, in the hot, outdated, 1970s-era Formica–linoleum–avocado green kitchen, I made loads of tomato pies, maybe even dozens. The recipe got splattered with tomato guts and mayonnaise—yes, there's mayonnaise, too, but only a third of a cup—the words smearing in spots. But it didn't matter, because by the end of the week I had made so many tomato pies, I knew the recipe by heart. The first layer of biscuit crust is covered with sliced fresh tomatoes, then sprinkled with chopped basil and topped with shredded cheddar cheese. A mixture of mayonnaise and lemon juice is then poured over the filling, which is covered with the second crust and baked until it's browned and bubbly. The smells of that pie on a hot summer day make you feel dizzy, so intoxicating are they.

No one in my family knew just how important that tomato pie was to me. Not just because it used the freshest ingredients at their prime deliciousness. Not just because eating tomato pie is something akin to reaching nirvana. Not even because it made me popular and made me look incredibly talented. No, this tomato pie was important to me because it wasn't just anybody's recipe, it was Laurie Colwin's recipe.

Is it possible that there are people out there who do not know Laurie Colwin's writing? Yes, she of the *Gourmet* magazine column in the 1990s. But also of eight books of fiction—short stories and novels. When I was working as a TWA flight attendant back in the late 1970s and early '80s and dreaming of becoming a writer, Laurie Colwin was one of my heroines. This was before the rented beach houses, and before her food writing, when her stories would appear like little jewels in *The New Yorker.* When I would read lines like these from "Mr. Parker": "He was very thin . . . but he was calm and cheery, in the way you expect plump people to be." Or: "As a girl she'd had bright red hair, which was now the color of old leaves." I would smile at just how perfect her descriptions were, and at how perfectly she captured real people. "I don't work. I'm lazy. I don't do anything very important . . . I just live day to day enjoying myself," a character tells us in Colwin's 1978 novel, *Happy All the Time*.

To me then—and still now—Laurie Colwin was a kind of Manhattan Jane Austen. Her novels and stories examined ordinary people and ordinary lives, the very kind of writing I wanted to do. Even though she tackled themes like marital love and familial love, themes that might be construed as sentimental, Colwin appreciated and plumbed the ambiguities of relationships, always turning a sharp eye on them. In *Happy All the Time*, her character Misty attends a dinner party with her fiancé: "How wonderful everything tasted, Misty thought. Everything had a sheen on it. Was that what love did, or was it merely the wine? She decided that it was love." But just when Colwin appears to be veering perhaps too near sentimentality, she throws a sharp observation at us. Misty also says: "You believe in happy endings. I don't. You think everything is going to work out fine. I don't. You think everything is ducky. I don't." She then goes on to explain: "I come from a family that fled the Czar's army, got their heads broken on picket lines, and has never slept peacefully anywhere." Colwin does this again and again in her fiction. In *A Big Storm Knocked It Over*, her posthumous 1993 novel, Jane Louise considers other women: "Their pinkness, their blondness, their carefully streaked hair, nail polish, eyelash curlers, mascara, the heap of things . . . that Jane Louise never used made her feel that they were women in a way that she was not." She was generous to her characters. And funny. And honest.

Although my family did not flee the czar's army or get our heads broken on picket lines, we were—like many in Colwin's fiction—a waiting-for-the-other-shoe-to-drop family. An aunt dead during a wisdom tooth extraction. An uncle dead on a dance floor on Valentine's night. But also like Colwin's characters, who find "the experience of having a baby exactly like being madly in love," as Billy does in *Another Marvelous Thing*, we love fiercely. And those weeks in those rented beach houses in the early 1990s could have, in many ways, stepped right out of *Happy All the Time*: "We're all together. We're family and we're friends. I think that's the best thing in the world."

I COME FROM a public beach kind of family—no pool clubs or private cabanas for us. Growing up, I spent most of my summers sweating in our backyard or watching game shows on TV, sitting in front of the fan and eating root beer ice pops. My mother worked at a candy factory, stuffing plastic Christmas stockings with cheap toys and candy all summer. But she got Fridays off, and she and my aunt would load us kids into one of their station wagons and drive down to Scarborough Beach, where my cousin Gloria-Jean and I sat on a separate blanket and pretended not to know the rest of the family. We had plans, big plans. To leave Rhode Island and our blue-collar, immigrant-Italian roots behind. Even at the beach, we toted Dickens or Austen, big fat books that helped the hot, humid summer pass.

I did escape. First to college, where I waitressed every summer at a tony beach club and studied how the women there held their fancy drinks—brandy Alexanders and Lillet with a twist of orange peel. I studied how they held themselves, too, the way they shrugged their sweaters from their shoulders directly into a man's waiting hands. The way they looked, a combination of boredom and amusement. Outside the club, their children learned how to play tennis and how to dive, how to order lunch from the guy at the grill and sign their parents' names and membership numbers on the bill.

In 1978 I became a flight attendant for TWA, a job I held for the next eight years, serving mostly businessmen in first class. In training we learned how to carve chateaubriand, dress lamb chops in foil stockings, mix a perfect martini. I developed a taste for the leftover caviar and the champagne from duty-free shops across Europe. Eventually I settled on Bleecker Street in New York City and fulfilled a dream I'd had since I'd read *Little Women* in second grade: I became a writer. As is often the case, with success came a longing for home. We yearn so much to leave our small town, our childhood home, the familiar. Yet somehow once we've left it all behind, it beckons us back. How I longed for the taste of my mother's meatballs; the casual way I would flop onto the couch beside my father, dropping my feet into his lap; the noisy nights around the kitchen table with all those loud, Pall Mall–smoking, black coffee–drinking relatives; the long, sandy beaches of Rhode Island with the smell of Coppertone, and clam cakes frying in oil mingling with the salty air. Of course I loved where I had landed, in a small apartment in NoHo, my books on bookstore shelves, my days spent writing, my nights at parties or readings, just as I'd imagined, or maybe hoped, when I'd dreamed of a writer's life. But I wanted home, too, and when I offered to rent a house at the beach, my parents assumed it would be at Scarborough.

Rhode Island has beautiful beaches with long stretches of sand and crashing waves. Isolated beaches and remote beaches and beaches that require special passes just to sit on them. Still, my parents wanted the state beach, so Scarborough is where we went. I brought lots of recipes with me that first summer, and for the dozen or so that followed. But it was the tomato pie that became a symbol of those weeks in that split-level ranch house across a busy road from the crowded beach. The more local tomatoes that appeared at the Stop & Shop, the more pies I made.

We ate the pies on the back deck of those houses—we never rented the same exact one, yet they were all identical, located in a treeless development called Eastward Look. We ate tomato pies with grilled cheeseburgers and hot dogs and Italian sausages, my father manning the grill with a cold beer in his hand. There were often dozens of us at dinner—cousins and aunts and uncles and the women from my mother's Friday night poker club. At some point, pasta (we called it *macaroni*) would be served. And meatballs and my Auntie Dora's

Italian meatloaf. The tomato pie appeared at lunch with the cold cuts and sometimes even at breakfast, heated up.

The soggy recipe page went back to my Greenwich Village apartment with me, but it returned to Rhode Island and that year's rented beach house every summer, growing more faded and smudged over time. That was okay; I needed only to glance it at to remind myself what temperature to bake it at (400 degrees) and how many lemons I needed for the juice to add to the mayo (just one). My father marveled at that pie. As a midwesterner, he always ate apple pie with cheddar cheese, and he liked that this pie had cheese in it. I admit, some of my relatives didn't like the tomato pie, or at least remained suspicious of it. But the beach house was so crowded, so full of family, of aunts and uncles and cousins and old friends and new husbands, that the response to the naysayers was just *More for us, then!*

THE FIRST TIME I saw Laurie Colwin was back in the 1980s, long before tomato pie, when I was working for TWA and writing what I thought were interconnected short stories (they later become my first novel). Colwin and Deborah Eisenberg were giving a reading at Three Lives bookstore, not far from my Bleecker Street apartment. In those days, *The New Yorker* ran two short stories a week, and sometimes the writers read together at Three Lives. I remember it as a January or February night, cold with an icy sleet falling as I made my way to the reading. I arrived late, or maybe just on time: they had not yet begun to read but a hush had already fallen over the packed store.

For a moment, I paused in the doorway and stared at the two women sitting together at the front of the crowd: Eisenberg, skinny and dark-haired, her legs folded up like origami; Colwin, curly-haired and plump and grinning. She looked up and I swear, in that moment, I thought she was grinning at me. I thought—and this sounds crazy, I know—but I thought she was beckoning me in, not just to the little bookstore but into this world of words and writers. A woman, annoyed, in charge, began waving her arms at me to come and sit. And then the irritated woman pointed at the only place left, which happened to be right at the feet of Laurie Colwin.

I believe that Colwin read something from what would become *Goodbye Without Leaving*, her novel about the only white backup singer in a touring soul group. But the memory is fuzzy. I really remember only the smells of steam heat and wet wool, the way the audience listened, rapt. I remember wanting to say something to Colwin, something about how her generous heart came through on the page, how happy I felt when I saw a new story by her. But I was too shy. I stood and watched people line up to speak to her, and to Eisenberg, to get books signed and shake hands. And then I left. As I walked back through that cold, icy night, something settled in me: I could do this. I could be a writer. No. I *would* be a writer. And as corny and impossible as it sounds, Laurie Colwin's smile, the one she sent to me that night, made it so.

THIS WAS ALL long before I discovered tomato pie. Before I started publishing stories and novels. Before I brought my family to those rented houses in Eastward Look for a few weeks each summer.

Over time, we stopped renting those beach houses at Scarborough Beach. My father got lung cancer, got sick, then sicker, then died. My aunts and uncles died, too. And my mother's Friday night poker club dwindled from twelve to nine to four as the women, too, died. Cousins moved away. New husbands became ex-husbands. And that recipe, the one torn from a long-ago *Gourmet,* got lost in the move from one apartment to another, or perhaps one city to another. Whenever we learn that someone we admired and loved died, we meet the news with disbelief. But perhaps even more so with Laurie Colwin's sudden death in October at only forty-eight from heart failure. Although I can't now recall where I first read about Colwin's death, her prescience only added to my stunned disbelief, because I did remember clearly how Mrs. Parker, in Colwin's 1973 short story "Mr. Parker," died suddenly in October of heart failure. Wrapped up in the heartbreak of a broken romance, I learned about it months later, in winter. Had it been summer, had I still owned that faded recipe, I would have made tomato pie the day I heard.

In the two decades since then, I have found and lost love and found it again. It has turned me to mush. I've published more than a dozen books. I've had three children, and lost one suddenly and horribly when she was only five. My heart has broken again and again, and miraculously it has healed. There have been so many things I didn't take good enough care of, or hold on to tight enough, because we don't really believe we will lose them, do we? Somehow we are always stunned that things go away, disappear, die. People, too. They leave us, and even though we know better, their leaving is always a surprise.

Then one summer day a few years ago, I line farm tomatoes up on my windowsill, I glimpse the basil taking over my yard, and I have one thought: tomato pie. Is it too much to hope that the recipe had found its way to the Internet? I type in "Laurie Colwin" and "tomato pie," and just like that I have it again, my beloved recipe, still the ripe tomatoes, still the basil and double biscuit crust, and, yes, one-third of a cup of mayonnaise.

I preheat the oven to 400 degrees. I cut into the tomatoes, letting their juice spill everywhere, and I remember that long-ago winter night when I stood in the doorway of Three Lives bookstore and Laurie Colwin smiled at me. I am smiling now, at her wherever she is, at all the people and all the things I've lost, because in that moment I feel like maybe we never really lose the things we love. Maybe they are still, somehow, close. I go into the yard and pluck the greenest, most tender leaves of basil and I hold them to my nose and breathe in, deep. In that instant, I am back at Scarborough Beach and the women of my mother's card club are all there, ready to throw their pennies onto the table, and my aunts are complaining about putting tomatoes in a pie and my father is grinning because there is cheddar cheese in it and the recipe is smeared but still readable and the tomatoes are so fresh and so red that I swear, there has never been anything that red since.

LAURIE COLWIN'S TOMATO PIE

I have seen many iterations of this recipe: with corn, with—God help us—goat cheese, without the biscuit crust. Colwin cites a woman named Mary who owned a tea shop in Salisbury, Connecticut, as her recipe's source, and I have, for the most part, stuck true to her version. Why mess with something perfect? However, a few years ago I was teaching in Chamonix, France, for several weeks and was asked to make tomato pie for a dinner party. The grocery store there had no cheddar cheese, no mayonnaise, and a measurement of baking powder that not even Google could translate. So I substituted: Gruyère for the cheddar and a Dijon mustard–mayo condiment for the straight mayo; I took my chances with the baking powder. The result was delicious. More sophisticated, perhaps, than the rustic original. Tangy and vaguely French, what with the Dijon and Gruyère. Although back home I returned to the original, I concede that other variations can suffice in a pinch. "It is hard to describe how delicious this [tomato pie] is," Colwin wrote in *More Home Cooking,* where the recipe appeared, "especially on a hot day with a glass of magnificent iced tea in a beautiful setting, but it would doubtless be just as scrumptious on a cold day in your warm kitchen with a cup of coffee."

INGREDIENTS

CRUST

2 cups all-purpose flour

1 stick butter

4 teaspoons baking powder

¾ cup milk

FILLING

*2 pounds fresh tomatoes, sliced thin, or, in winter, two 28-
    ounce cans of good canned tomatoes, drained and sliced thin*

3 to 4 tablespoons chopped basil, chives, or scallions

1½ cups grated sharp cheddar cheese

⅓ cup mayonnaise

2 tablespoons lemon juice

1. Preheat the oven to 400 degrees F.
2. To make the double biscuit crust, blend by hand or in a food processor the flour, butter, baking powder, and milk.
3. Roll half of the dough on a floured surface and fit into a 9-inch pie plate.
4. Lay the tomatoes over the crust and scatter basil, chives, or scallions over them.

5. Sprinkle 1 cup of the shredded cheddar over the tomatoes.

6. Thin the mayonnaise with the lemon juice and drizzle it over the tomatoes and cheese.

7. Cover with the remaining cheddar cheese.

8. Roll out the remaining crust and fit it over the top, sealing the edges and cutting steam slits.

9. Bake for 25 minutes.

10. This pie can be made ahead and reheated at 350 degrees F till gooey.

Acknowledgments

I am the luckiest writer around and so grateful for my agent, Gail Hochman, and everyone at Brandt & Hochman, as well as my editor Jill Bialosky, my publicist Erin Lovett, and everyone at W. W. Norton. Lucky and grateful, too, for my wonderful kids, Sam and Annabelle, who support and indulge their writer mom. Thank you to my love, my husband, Michael Ruhlman, who makes every day happy. It breaks my heart that my mom, Gogo, didn't live to see this book in print. But her fingerprints are on every page, and on my heart.

Some of the essays appeared in earlier publications:

"The Golden Silver Palate" in *Alimentum* and in *Best Food Writing 2011*

"The Best Fried Chicken" in *Riverteeth*

"Love, Lunch, and Meatball Grinders" in *Parade*

"Confessions of a Marsha Jordan Girl" in *Yankee*

"My Father's Pantry" in *Tin House*

"Party Like It's 1959" in *Food & Wine*

"How to Butcher a Pig" in *Rhode Island Monthly*

"How to Smoke Salmon" in *Brainchild*

"The Summer of Omelets" in *Brainchild*

"Tomato Pie" in *Tin House* and in *Best Food Writing 2014*

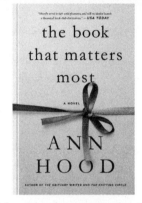
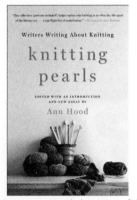